Y0-AKW-855

© Copyright 1984 by Broekmans & Van Poppel B.V., Amsterdam, unless stated otherwise.

Niets uit deze uitgave mag worden verveelvoudigd en/of openbaar gemaakt worden door middel van druk, fotokopie, microfilm of op welke andere wijze ook, zonder voorafgaande schriftelijke toestemming van de uitgever.
No part of this book may be reproduced in any form by print, photoprint, microfilm or any other means without written permission from the publisher.

Graphic design Marc Terstroet

Druk: Drukkerij S.J.P. Bakker B.V., Badhoevedorp.

Concerning the Flute

Ten articles about flute literature, flute playing, flute making and flutists by Jane Bowers, Nikolaus Delius, David Lasocki, Karl Lenski, Betty Bang Mather, Peter van Munster, Mirjam Nastasi, Rineke Smilde, Karl Ventzke and Frans Vester.

Edited by Rien de Reede

ML45
55
V39
1984

This book is dedicated to Frans Vester and was presented to him on the occasion of his retirement from the Royal Conservatory in The Hague, June 15th 1984.

Frans Vester

Contents

Peter van Munster
Frans Vester, 'een geleerd musicus' — 9
Frans Vester, a 'learned musician' — 29

Jane M. Bowers
The Hotteterre family of woodwind instrument makers — 33

Betty Bang Mather
The performance of trills in french baroque dance music — 55

David Lasocki
A new look at the life of John Loeillet (1680-1730) — 65

Nikolaus Delius
Die Flötenkonzerte von Pietro Nardini — 75

Mirjam Nastasi
John Gunn's 'The Art of Playing the German Flute on New Principles', London 1793 — 81

Karl Ventzke
F.L. Dulon, der blinde Flötenspieler (1769-1826). Über 'Leben und Meynungen' eines reisenden Virtuosen — 91

Karl Lenski
Bilitis: eine beinahe vergessene Liebe von Claude Debussy — 107

Rineke Smilde
De musicq lievende werd bekend gemaekt... — 115

Frans Vester
Publishers, Editors, Editions and Urtexts — 121

Frans Vester,
'een geleerd musicus'

Peter van Munster

Weemoedige gevoelens op 9-jarige leeftijd zijn verantwoordelijk voor de keus van Frans Vester voor de fluit. Had hij toen niet het boek *Ver van huis*, uitgegeven bij Callenbach in Nijkerk, gelezen, het huidige Nederlandse muziekleven zou er anders hebben uitgezien.
Het verhaal ging over twee jongetjes die in Nederland op school gingen en waarvan de ouders in het verre Indië verbleven. De jongste van de twee had een blokfluit. Als hij daar op speelde leefde hij in zijn eigen wereld en vergat hij zijn heimwee.
Hoewel Frans veilig samen met zijn ouders en zijn zuster in Beverwijk woonde vond hij deze geschiedenis zo mooi dat hij besloot fluit te gaan spelen.

Frans Vester, geboren op 22 mei 1922 in Den Haag, verhuisde op zijn zevende jaar naar Beverwijk. Zijn vader, fotolithograaf op een blikfabriek in Krommenie, speelde voor zijn plezier viool en stimuleerde Frans' interesse voor de muziek door hem te laten proberen op de piano Mozartsonates te begeleiden. Eerst alleen een paar noten met de linkerhand, daarna spelenderwijs meer.
De fluitlessen naar aanleiding van *Ver van huis* begonnen op 10-jarige leeftijd. Aanvankelijk gedurende een jaar bij een amateur fluitist/hoboïst, daarna bij de in Haarlem wonende musicus en muziekcriticus Jos de Klerk. De uit België afkomstige De Klerk was een veelzijdig man. Hij had in Antwerpen fluit, zang en compositie gestudeerd en was in 1918 naar Nederland uitgeweken. Hij was kennelijk geïnteresseerd in de kleine Vester. De wekelijkse les van een uur liep uit tot hele zaterdagmiddagen waarop niet alleen het fluitspel aan de orde kwam, maar ook harmonie, solfège, algemene muziekleer en instrumentatie. Kosten: één rijksdaalder.
De vier jaar die Vester bij Jos de Klerk doorbracht zijn van grote vormende betekenis geweest. Samen bezochten ze de concerten van de Haarlemsche Orkest Vereniging (het huidige Noordhollands Filharmonisch Orkest) waarbij Frans, 11 jaar oud, de blaadjes van de partituren moest omslaan en zodoende leerde lezen en luisteren. Ook liet De Klerk hem aan de hand van pianouittreksels de orkestratie van operafragmenten reconstrueren. Later werd dat dan vergeleken met het origineel.
Wat muziekgeschiedenis betreft las Vester alles wat hij maar te pakken kon krijgen. Pianoles kreeg hij van iemand in Beverwijk. Ondertussen bezocht hij na de lagere school de ULO (school voor Uitgebreid Lager Onderwijs), die hij evenwel niet afmaakte omdat hij in 1937, 15 jaar oud, toelatingsexamen deed aan het Amsterdams Conservatorium en onmiddellijk werd toegelaten. Zijn nieuwe leraar werd Hubert Barwahser, eerste fluitist van het Concertgebouworkest en enige fluitleraar aan het conservatorium waar overigens niet meer dan vier of vijf hoofdvakleerlingen waren.
Tijdens zijn conservatoriumperiode bleek Vester hoe belangrijk de vier jaren daarvoor waren geweest. Jos de Klerk besteedde aan toonvorming niet veel aandacht, maar had hem naast de gebruikelijke Bach-Händel-Mozart stukken het gehele romantisch-virtuoze fluitrepertoire van

Berbiguier, Drouet en Fürstenau tot Boehm, Doppler en Demersseman laten doorwerken, onder het motto 'in het water leer je zwemmen'. Op het conservatorium kwam daar geen verandering in. Toen Vester in 1941 eindexamen deed met het Concert in G van Mozart begeleid door het conservatoriumorkest o.l.v. directeur Willem Andriessen, had hij het gevoel niet verder gekomen te zijn dan het peil waarop hij bij zijn toelatingsexamen was. Zijn belangstelling voor de fluit was verflauwd, alleen zijn interesse voor de piano was toegenomen, mede dank zij de lessen van bijvakleraar Karel de Jong.

Pas na de oorlog, door het luisteren via de radio naar grammofoonplaten van de Franse fluitist Marcel Moyse, begon Vester de fluit weer mooi te vinden. Moyse's uitvoeringen van het Concert in D van Mozart, de Sonate La Vibray van Blavet en de Triosonate van Bach (met Blanche Honegger, viool en Louis Moyse, piano) brachten hem aan het denken en zetten hem op een nieuw spoor. Hij werd een bewonderaar van het Franse fluitspel.

Orkesten

Al vanaf zijn dertiende jaar speelde Vester van tijd tot tijd bij de Haarlemsche Orkest Vereniging, bijvoorbeeld wanneer daar de Suite in b.kl.t. van J.S. Bach met niet minder dan zes fluiten werd uitgevoerd. In 1939 verving hij bij hetzelfde orkest als tweede fluitist voor een half jaar Dick Kuiper (later fluitist bij het Concertgebouworkest en thans fluitbouwer in Nederhorst den Berg) die in dienst moest. In 1941 trad Vester definitief in dienst van de H.O.V. Salaris: ƒ 17,85 per week. Omdat er maar twee fluitisten in vaste dienst waren moest hij bij de grotere werken een keus maken uit het spelen van de tweede fluitpartij of de piccolopartij, waardoor er altijd wat weg bleef.

Voor het orkest stond Toon Verhey, een geniaal dirigent die alles uit het hoofd deed en niet rustte voor zijn klankvoorstelling gerealiseerd was. Van zijn ideeën over frasering, hoogtepunten, weten wanneer een noot kort of lang moet zijn, leerde Vester veel.

Na een verbintenis van één maand, in 1942, bij het Residentieorkest, werd Vester van hogerhand overgeplaatst naar het Utrechts Stedelijk Orkest. Daar kwam hij in de plaats van Piet van den Hurk die wegens anti-Duitse uitlatingen was opgepakt. Een half jaar later volgde er een samenvoeging met het Omroeporkest tot het orkest van de *Reichssender in den Niederlanden*, een week later meldde Vester zich ziek en werd op grond van vermeende maagklachten afgekeurd. Om aan de *Arbeitseinsatz* te ontkomen liet hij zich inschrijven als compositiestudent aan het conservatorium in Den Haag, waar hij een half jaar les had van Henk Badings. Te kort om te leren componeren maar lang genoeg om nieuwe ideeën over muziek op te doen. Wie Vester naar zijn toenmalige composities vraagt krijgt een minachtend 'waardeloos' te horen. Dat neemt niet weg dat zijn hoboconcert en stukken voor trompet en piano indertijd met plezier door de spelers zijn uitgevoerd.

Na de oorlog, in september 1945, kwam hij voor de derde maal in dienst bij de H.O.V., nu als eerste fluitist. Het orkest was uitgebreid, de grotere werken van Ravel, Bruckner en Strauss konden in de volledige bezetting worden uitgevoerd. Vester trad een paar maal als solist op met concerten van Vivaldi en Mozart; niet zijn eerste solistische activiteiten overigens. Al als 19-jarige had hij met de H.O.V. de eerste uitvoering in Nederland gegeven van het fluitconcert van Jacques Ibert. De primitieve werkwijze van het orkest, 'openluchtconcerten en zo', bracht hem er toe na één seizoen ontslag te nemen. Korte tijd later, eind 1946, trad Vester in dienst van de Nederlandse Radio Unie als tweede fluitist van het Radiokamerorkest. Dit hield hij twee jaar vol en verliet toen spoorslags Hilversum. In 1953 keerde hij er terug na de vraag 'of hij het prettig zou vinden eerste fluitist van het Promenadeorkest te worden'. Dit kon hij niet weigeren.

Dirigent van het Promenadeorkest was Benedict Silbermann, iemand die in staat was een hele ochtend op de Radetzky-mars te werken alsof het een symfonie van Brahms was. Volgens Vester, die daar wel waardering voor had, werd hem dat niet door alle musici in dank afgenomen. De vreemde arrangementen bij het Promenadeorkest, waarbij de fluit veel en snel in het hoge register werd gebruikt, vereisten een grote handigheid en een perfecte techniek. Vester, die zich nooit om techniek had bekommerd en zelfs beweert op het conservatorium nooit te hebben gestudeerd, merkte dat dingen die vroeger als vanzelf gingen plotseling gestudeerd moesten worden. Hier deden zich voor het eerst de problemen met de linkerhand voor die zich jaren later veel duidelijker zouden manifesteren. Mogelijkheden om met het Promenadeorkest solo te spelen waren er te over. Ze varieerden van uitzendingen van het Concert in D van Mozart en het Concertino van Chaminade tot en met amusement-achtige composities met combo.

Ook met de andere radio-orkesten trad Vester regelmatig op, zoals met het Radio Filharmonisch Orkest waarmee hij Concerten van Mozart (in G), Pendleton, Nielsen en Ibert uitvoerde. Het aantal verschillende concerten voor fluit en orkest dat hij in de loop van zijn carrière heeft gespeeld bedraagt volgens zijn eigen telling 65.

Drang naar verandering en onvrede met de Hilversumse sfeer voerden Vester in 1955 naar Amsterdam, waar hij eerste fluitist bij het orkest van de Nederlandse Opera werd. Een baan met veel perspectieven ten aanzien van het ontplooien van activiteiten buiten het orkest. Iedere eerste lessenaar was dubbel bezet zodat er in feite maar een halve dienst gespeeld hoefde te worden. Dat leverde een hoeveelheid vrije tijd op waarvan we rustig kunnen aannemen dat Vester die niet verlummelde. Niet iedereen was het daar mee eens, gezien de ironische ansichtkaart uit het buitenland van de dirigent Peter Maag aan de leden van het operaorkest, geschreven nadat er ongetwijfeld strubbelingen op het arbeidsvoorwaardenvlak aan vooraf waren gegaan. De tekst luidde 'van harte gefeliciteerd met het bereiken van de één-urige werkweek'.

Dat Vester zijn tijd niet verdeed blijkt wel uit zijn werkzaamheden bij het Nederlands Kamerorkest die ongeveer tegelijkertijd begonnen. Het Nederlands Kamerorkest werd in het leven geroepen door de toenmalige directeur van het Holland Festival, Peter Diamand, en was voornamelijk bedoeld om, naast optreden in het festival, via buitenlandse tournees de naam van Nederland te propageren. De basis bestond uit een vaste groep strijkers, waaronder concertmeester Willem Noske, de cellisten Piet Lentz en Anner Bijlsma en de bassist Anthony Woodrow. Vaste claveciniste was Janny van Wering. De blazers werden per keer gecontracteerd. Gedurende twee jaar maakte Vester regelmatig deel uit van dit ensemble. De tournees brachten hem o.a. in Griekenland, Italië en Engeland, waar hij tijdens het Edinburgh Festival samen met de fluitist Johan Feltkamp het vierde Brandenburgse Concert van Bach speelde. Het orkest werd geleid, al spelende, door de uit Polen afkomstige violist Szymon Goldberg. Vooral op het gebied van concentratie en ensemblespel was dit iemand van wie Vester veel leerde. Uit deze tijd stammen ook de eerste contacten met Anner Bijlsma met wie ideeën over muziek en over speurwerk in bibliotheken werden uitgewisseld.

Terug naar de opera. Van tijd tot tijd viel hier muzikaal ook nog wel eens wat te beleven. Volgens Vester het meest bij de routine-dirigenten, mensen die hun vak goed verstonden zoals b.v. Arrigo Guarnieri. Hoogtepunten waren opera's van Janacek onder Jaroslav Krumbholz en The Rake's Progress van Strawinsky onder Erich Leinsdorf. Het spelen in de bak was natuurlijk niet het meest opwindende wat een musicus kon overkomen, maar opera's als Carmen van Bizet en Figaro's Hochzeit en Don Giovanni van Mozart waren voor een fluitist toch leuk om te

doen. Wel stoorde Vester zich toen al aan bepaalde stijlloze opvattingen.
Tijdens de periode bij de opera werd het Danzi Kwintet opgericht, waarover later meer. Vester bleef bij de opera tot aan de opheffing in 1966.

Kamermuziek

Op het Amsterdams Conservatorium waar Vester in de jaren '37-'41 verbleef was nog geen sprake van enig onderwijs op kamermuziekgebied. De school was er in de eerste plaats op gericht om orkestmusici op te leiden. Zelfs het idee later leraar te worden zou menigeen belachelijk voorgekomen zijn. De z.g. voordrachtsoefeningen, waarop Vester wel eens een duetje speelde, waren hoge uitzonderingen.

Frans Vester en Miep van Luin

Zijn eerste serieuze verrichtingen op het terrein van de kamermuziek ontstonden in de oorlog, in Haarlem, in de kringen van de H.O.V. Daar bleef het fluit-pianoduo Frans Vester-Miep van Luin uit over dat tussen 1945 en 1955 regelmatig, en daarna wat incidenteler, optrad. Het repertoire bestond aanvankelijk uit gangbare werken als de Sonate van Hindemith, Joueurs de flûte van Roussel, de Variaties van Schubert en de Sonate van Pijper, maar op den duur werden nieuwere stukken gespeeld w.o. de Sonate van Prokofiev (eerste uitvoering in Nederland), de Sonates van Martinu en Leibowitz tot en met de Sonatine van Boulez die in 1959 in het Stedelijk Museum in Amsterdam in première ging. De optredens in het Stedelijk Museum waren te danken aan Daniel Ruyneman die daar op zondagmiddagen concerten verzorgde met hedendaagse muziek in het kader van zijn 'Society for Contemporary Music'. Het duo trad verder op door het hele land voor volksuniversiteiten en kunstkringen en enige malen in Parijs, Brussel en Antwerpen. De bewerkingen die Vester voor fluit en piano maakte van een aantal stukjes 'für die Flötenuhr' van Haydn waren kleine juweeltjes die bij het publiek zeer in de smaak vielen.

Het eerste kamermuziekensemble waarvan Vester tijdens zijn periode bij de radio deel uit maakte was het Radio Cembalo Gezelschap, dat verder bestond uit Cor Coppens, hobo, Henk de Blij, viool, Dick Vos, altviool, Wil Strieder, cello en Janny van Wering, clavecimbel. Met dit ensemble werden bijna wekelijks radiouitzendingen met oude muziek verzorgd. Van een veranderende stijlopvatting was nog geen sprake, dat gebeurde pas bij *Arte Fiato*, een trio dat Vester oprichtte samen met twee collega's uit het Promenadeorkest, de hoboïst Koen van Slogteren en de fagottist Arnold Swillens. Het repertoire voor deze combinatie was beperkt zodat al snel naar uitbreiding werd gezocht. Het clavecimbel bleek de oplossing omdat het met de fagot de rol van basso continuo kon vervullen. Er werd contact gezocht met de clavecinist Hans Brandts Buys, die positief reageerde. Brandts Buys was in die tijd een pionier op het gebied van oude muziek. Hij was directeur van het Muzieklyceum in Hilversum en dirigent van een studentenkoor en -orkest in Utrecht, het USKO, waar hij Bach-cantates mee uitvoerde. Hij publiceerde veel, vooral over Bach, en was evenals Vester een verwoed kopiïst van muziek. Hij hield zich op wetenschappelijke wijze met o.a. historische uitvoeringspraktijk bezig, waardoor hij in ieder geval zeker wist dat wat er tot dan toe gebeurde op dat gebied zeer aanvechtbaar was. Hij bezat een enorme bibliotheek waaruit Vester naar hartelust kon lenen en kopiëren.

Na een jaar lang wekelijks 4 à 5 keer intensief gerepeteerd te hebben, waarbij veel gediscussieerd werd over interpretatie en de uitvoering van b.v. vrije versieringen, werd op 1 oktober 1953 het eerste concert gegeven in het Studenten Sanatorium in Laren. Behalve triosonates en solosonates werd daar ook een versie gespeeld van het eerste Londoner Trio van Joseph Haydn voor fluit, hobo en fagot. Arte Fiato heeft bestaan tot 1959 en speelde in binnen- en buitenland, ondermeer voor de B.B.C. in Londen en voor de Belgische Radio. De muziekcriticus Lex van Delden schreef in 1965 in Het Parool:
Hoed af voor de voortreffelijke blazers die Nederland bezit! Hoe voortreffelijke er onder hen schuilen, bleek gisteravond weer in de goed bezette Kleine Zaal van Amsterdams Concertgebouw, waar het jonge ensemble Arte Fiato hartverwarmende bewijzen van meesterschap en bruisende musiceerkunst leverde. En zoveel succes oogstte dat het in den beginne gewoon-hartelijke applaus van lieverlede in een opgetogen demonstratie van ovaties verkeerde...

Een belangrijk ensemble dat zich na de oorlog met oude muziek bezig hield was Musica Antiqua bestaande uit Johan Feltkamp, fluit, Nicolaas Roth, viool, Hans Brandts Buys, clavecimbel en Carel van Leeuwen Boomkamp, cello. Via Brandts Buys en Van Leeuwen Boomkamp lopen lijnen naar Vester en Bijlsma, die later op hun beurt door contacten met Frans Brüggen en Gustav Leonhardt hebben bijgedragen tot de specifieke opvattingen over het spelen van oude muziek zoals die gaandeweg geaccepteerd zijn.

Het idee om te onderzoeken hoe 18e eeuwse muziek op de oorspronkelijke instrumenten geklonken moet hebben heeft ook Vester al in een vroeg stadium bezig gehouden. Naast zijn gewone werk begon hij uit experimenteerlust en als een soort uitdaging aan zichzelf op de traverso te studeren. Hij waagde het zelfs, ergens in het begin van de jaren vijftig, via een direkte radio-uitzending de Partita voor fluit solo van J.S. Bach uit te voeren. Veel later, in 1973, nam hij met het Mozart Ensemble Amsterdam, o.l.v. Frans Brüggen, de Concerten in G en D, het Concert voor fluit en harp in C (met Edward Witsenburg, harp), het Andante in C en het Rondo in D van Mozart voor de grammofoonplaat op, geheel op authentieke instrumenten gespeeld.

Vester ontmoette Brüggen voor het eerst in 1952 tijdens een huisconcert in Heemstede. Brüggen, 18 jaar oud, wilde voor eigen rekening een concert met fluit en blokfluit organiseren in de kleine zaal van het Amsterdams Concertgebouw en vroeg Vester daaraan mee te werken. Dat is het begin geweest van een langdurig contact waarbij veel over muziek werd gepraat maar ook menigmaal het spannende spel *Stap op* gespeeld werd, een soort kwartetspel waarbij een jongetje op de fiets naar bos en hei wordt gestuurd en de spelers elkaar d.m.v. tegenwind-, lekke band- en spoorwegovergangkaarten dwars kunnen zitten.

Dat Bach altijd 'fout' was gespeeld was voor menigeen zo langzamerhand wel duidelijk. Het besef drong door dat zoiets met Mozart ook wel eens het geval zou kunnen zijn. De mensen die zich daarmee bezig hielden en waarmee Vester nauw contact had waren, naast Brüggen: Gustav Leonhardt, Anner Bijlsma en Jaap Schröder. Met hen heeft Vester op kamermuziekgebied veel samengewerkt en een aantal grammofoonplaten opgenomen waaronder Fluitkwartetten van Mozart, Cantates van Bach en de Tafelmusik van Telemann.

Een uitgebreide lijst met opnamen op kamermuziek-gebied is te vinden onder het hoofdstuk 'Discografie'.

In 1967 ontstond een nieuw ensemble bestaande uit Frans Vester, traverso, Jaap Schröder, barokviool, Veronica Hampe, gamba en Anneke Uittenbosch, clavecimbel. Het kreeg aanvankelijk de naam 'Diapason 422' maar vanwege de onbekendheid van dat woord in het buitenland werd dat veranderd in *Estro Armonico Amsterdam*. Het ensemble trad op in buitenlandse steden waaronder Parijs, Londen, Heidelberg en Rome. In Nederland was het spelen op oude instrumenten al min of meer gemeengoed geworden, in het buitenland leverden de concerten van 'Estro Armonico' nog vaak verraste kritieken op. Het ensemble heeft bestaan tot 1973.

Hoe zijn Vesters opvattingen over het spelen van oude muziek ontstaan? Behalve door uitwisseling van ideeën met andere musici in de eerste plaats door veel te lezen. De oude bronnen zijn daarbij volgens Vester het meest betrouwbaar. Quantz' *Versuch einer Anweisung die Flöte traversière zu spielen* is naar zijn mening zeer waardevol voor de interpretatie van de muziek van Mozart. Van de hedendaagse auteurs noemt hij als eerste Sol Babitz, die de ideeën over het spelen van oude muziek het best heeft samengevat in een artikel 'The Great Baroque Hoax', geschreven in het door hemzelf uitgeven tijdschrift *The Early Music Laboratory Bulletin*. Als ander belangwekkend artikel van Babitz noemt hij 'Modern Errors in Mozart Performance' verschenen in het *Mozart-Jahrbuch 1967*. Hoe uiteenlopend de interpretatie van het notenbeeld in de verschillende stijltijdperken geweest is, een onderwerp dat Vester zeer na aan het hart ligt, wordt goed beschreven in *Notenschrift und Musizieren* van Willy Tappolet, een uitgave van Lienau (1967).

De laatste jaren is Vester meer en meer tot de overtuiging gekomen dat de beste manier om je zo wezenlijk mogelijk met muziek bezig te houden is om er niet zelf spelend bij betrokken te zijn, b.v. via het leiding geven aan ensembles. Vesters problemen met zijn slecht functionerende linkerhand zullen zijn opvattingen in die richting alleen maar versterkt hebben.
Dat heeft hem er niet van weerhouden om in 1980 het *Harmonicon Ensemble* op te richten dat naast hemzelf bestaat uit Jacques Holtman, viool, Jürgen Kussmaul, altviool, Anner Bijlsma, cello, Anthony Woodrow, contrabas, Han de Vries, hobo, Piet Honingh, klarinet, Brian Pollard, fagot, Vicente Zarzo, hoorn en Gérard van Blerk, piano. Dit ensemble is ontstaan uit de wens van Vester om grote romantische kamermuziekwerken, zoals het Septet van Hummel of het Nonet van Spohr uit te voeren.

Het Danzi Kwintet

Het blaaskwintet opus 26 van Arnold Schönberg, waarvan Vester vlak na de oorlog een zakpartituur in handen kreeg, is de aanleiding geweest tot de oprichting van het Danzi Kwintet in 1956. Deze compositie, in 1924 geschreven, was nog nooit in Nederland uitgevoerd en zag er op het eerste gezicht onspeelbaar uit. Vester schreef de partituur over op groter formaat en droeg het plan om het ooit nog eens te spelen, tien jaar met zich mee. Pas na zijn aanstelling bij de Opera in Amsterdam vond hij de juiste mensen die bereid waren dit voor die tijd ambitieuze plan te verwezenlijken. Dat waren aanvankelijk de hoboïst Leo Driehuis en de klarinettist Pem Godrie, beiden collega's uit het operaorkest, en twee leden van het Concertgebouworkest, de fagottist Brian Pollard en de hoornist Adriaan van Woudenberg. Van oprichting van een 'kwintet voor het leven' was nog geen sprake, het enige doel was de uitvoering van Schönbergs opus 26.
Zo werd in april 1958 in Pulchri te Den Haag het Nederlandse publiek geconfronteerd met de première van Schönbergs blaaskwintet en tevens met een nieuw Nederlands ensemble dat zich

inmiddels *Danzi Quintet* had genoemd. Het honorarium bedroeg ƒ 15,- per man en is nog steeds niet uitbetaald. Leo Driehuis, wiens ambities meer naar het dirigeren uitgingen, stapte kort daarna op. Hij werd opgevolgd door Koen van Slogteren die ook aan de Opera was verbonden. In de nieuwe bezetting traden 'de Danzi's' in de zomer van 1958 in het Holland Festival op. Ze speelden o.a. de kwintetten van Pijper en Schönberg en behaalden een overweldigend succes. Vanaf dat moment wisten ze zich verzekerd van grote belangstelling, ook van buitenlandse zijde. Het bleek dat er bij het concertpubliek een onvermoede behoefte bestond zowel aan hedendaagse muziek als aan een ander ensemble dan het gerenommeerde symfonieorkest of het ingeburgerde strijkkwartet.
Het Danzi Kwintet zag perspectieven en besloot te blijven bestaan. Vijf jaar later schreef Henk de By in Vrij Nederland:
Het Danzi Kwintet heeft op intelligente wijze van de nieuwe mogelijkheden profijt getrokken. Het heeft, vooral door de persoon van zijn primarius, de fluitist Frans Vester, op bijna wetenschappelijke wijze de recherche naar oude literatuur geopend (...) Belangrijker nog dan dit succesvolle onderzoek naar de bronnen van de blaaskwintetcultuur is hun inzet voor de muziek van onze tijd. (april 1963) (Uit *In plaats van applaus*. Uitg. Bakker/Daamen)
Inderdaad was het repertoire van het kwintet de eerste vijf jaar overwegend hedendaags. Dat vereiste een intensieve voorbereiding. Aan de première van Schönberg waren ongeveer honderd repetities voorafgegaan. Later werden nieuwe en ogenschijnlijk evenzeer onspeelbare werken op het repertoire genomen, zoals *Zeitmasse* van Karlheinz Stockhausen, een vele malen moeilijker partituur dan die van Schönberg. De Nederlandse première ervan vond plaats in 1960 waarbij de althobopartij gespeeld werd door Jaap Stotijn.

De keuze voor de hedendaagse muziek, samen met de grote inzet van de spelers, is de kracht geweest waardoor het Danzi Kwintet zich ontwikkelde tot een ensemble dat, ook internationaal gezien, op eenzame hoogte stond. Het idee om blaaskwintet te gaan spelen was op zich niet nieuw. In Nederland bestonden al het Haags Blaasquintet, het Concertgebouw Quintet en het Radio Philharmonisch Sextet (kwintet met piano). Ook in het buitenland waren voorbeelden te vinden, zoals het Quintette à Vent Française, het Dennis Brain Woodwind Quintet, het kwintet van Baden-Baden en het New York Woodwind Quintet. Voor al deze ensembles gold dat het kwintet spelen als iets naast het eigenlijke werk werd beschouwd, terwijl bij Vester en ook bij Van Slogteren het idee geleefd heeft om zich uiteindelijk los te maken uit de orkestpraktijk en van het kwintet hun belangrijkste bestaansmogelijkheid te maken. Die mogelijkheid heeft zich inderdaad een paar keer voorgedaan. De Folkwangschule in Essen bijvoorbeeld, had belangstelling. Daar zouden de Danzi's als musici 'in residence' naast hun lessen aan dat instituut alle tijd gehad hebben voor hun eigen ontwikkeling en hun tournees. Ook uit Amerika en Israël kwamen dergelijke voorstellen. De stap bleek echter te groot en te onzeker voor de andere kwintetleden, het ging niet door. Voor Vester is dat een teleurstelling geweest. Hij had graag vanuit een dergelijk verband tot een beter niveau van spelen willen komen.
De bezetting onderging in de loop van de 22 jaar dat het kwintet bestaan heeft nog enige malen een wijziging. Na zes jaar verliet Pem Godrie het ensemble. Zijn plaats werd ingenomen door Piet Honingh, klarinettist van het Concertgebouworkest, die bleef tot aan de opheffing in 1978. Koen van Slogteren, die ook de organisatie voor het grootste gedeelte verzorgde, verdween na twaalf jaar en werd opgevolgd door achtereenvolgens Maarten Karres, Han de Vries en Jan Spronk.
Wat de tournees betreft was Duitsland het eerste en vervolgens jaarlijkse uitstapje. Daarna volgden o.a. Israël, Polen, Engeland, Amerika en, op voorspraak van Kirill Kondrasjin,

Rusland. Kondrasjin, die op dat moment als gastdirigent voor het Concertgebouworkest stond en in de U.S.S.R. een hoge plaats in het muziekleven innam, vond dat de Russische blazers nog wel wat van hun Nederlandse collega's konden leren. Het Danzi Kwintet nam de invitatie aan op voorwaarde dat ze vrij moesten zijn in hun programmakeuze. Zo werd voor een enthousiast publiek in Moskou het kwintet van Schönberg gespeeld en werden de Danzi's tot hun verbazing tot ereleden van de Bond van Sovjet-musici benoemd. In Moskou ontstond het contact met de belangrijke componist Edison Denisov, die voor hen een kwintet schreef, een zeer geavanceerd en gecompliceerd werk.

Tijdens de tournees door Amerika, waar de belangstelling voor blazersensembles in het algemeen groot is, werd niet alleen geconcerteerd maar ook aan verschillende universiteiten les gegeven. Dit leverde weer een aantal voor het kwintet geschreven nieuwe partituren op, die echter lang niet allemaal gespeeld zijn; het was niet meer bij te houden.

In Oostenrijk, in Alpbach, ontstond in 1961 het contact met Karlheinz Stockhausen, die na het horen van het Danzi Kwintet, volgens eigen zeggen zijn angst voor het blaaskwintet kwijtgeraakt was. Hij nodigde hen uit in zijn nabijgelegen vakantieverblijf nog wat meer te laten horen. De enigszins overmoedig geworden kwintetleden besloten een werk van Michael Haydn voor hem te spelen dat toch nog gerepeteerd moest worden en waar de tijd voor had ontbroken. Stockhausen hoorde het aan, zei: 'Scheisse' en gaf het kwintet vervolgens een enige uren durend lesje in het spelen van oude muziek. Daarna werden nog wat experimenten gedaan op het gebied van de klankmogelijkheden, waarna Stockhausen toezegde een blaaskwintet te zullen schrijven en dit per minuut af te zullen leveren. Het stuk zou vanaf de eerste minuut uitgevoerd kunnen worden, iedere minuut kon er later aangeplakt worden. Hij is zijn belofte niet nagekomen. Wel heeft deze ontmoeting geleid tot het ontstaan van 'Abschied' voor blaaskwintet.

De grote invloed van het Danzi Kwintet op het Nederlandse muziekleven blijkt wel uit het indrukwekkende aantal composities dat aan het ensemble is opgedragen. De eerste voor hen geschreven werken waren 'Antiphonie', voor blaaskwintet en vier klanksporen van Ton de Leeuw en 'Improvisations and Symphonies' van Peter Schat, beide uit 1960. Daarna volgt een lange reeks composities van o.a. Kees van Baaren, Rudolf Escher, Hans Henkemans, Carel Brons, David Porcelijn, Jan van Vlijmen, Will Eisma, Jan Wisse, Rob du Bois, Otto Ketting, Guillaume Landré, Robert de Roos, Misha Mengelberg en Daniel Ruyneman.

Een andere, hoewel minder duidelijk aanwijsbare invloed is afkomstig van het succes dat het Danzi Kwintet oogstte met het hedendaagse repertoire. Dit moet voor de gevestigde symfonieorkesten en voor andere ensembles een stimulans geweest zijn hun eigen, vaak nogal behoudende, programmering te herzien. Ook het idee van subsidiëring van kamermuziek is in de Danzi-gelederen geboren. Het zijn Frans Vester en Koen van Slogteren geweest die als eersten naar het Ministerie van O.K. en W. stapten om een dergelijke subsidie te bepleiten. Aan de hand van statistieken konden ze aantonen dat de inkomsten in geen verhouding stonden tot de hoeveelheid tijd die in hun werk geïnvesteerd werd. Het Danzi Kwintet en het Nederlands Strijkkwartet zijn de eerste kamermuziekensembles geweest die door het Rijk financieel gesteund werden.

De angst voor verstarring die Vester in het verleden behoed had te lang bij een-en-hetzelfde orkest te blijven hangen, sloeg ook na tien jaar Danzi Kwintet toe. Het pakte positief uit doordat het hem op het idee bracht op oude instrumenten te gaan spelen. De instrumenten werden geleend door het Haags Gemeentemuseum op voorwaarde dat er een concert in het museum op zou volgen. Dat concert vond na een jaar studeren plaats. Als toegift werd een toonladder gespeeld zoals die klonk toen ze het jaar daarvoor begonnen waren. Erbarmelijk! De overschakeling op authentieke instrumenten bleek namelijk zeer ingrijpend te zijn. De stemming en onderlinge klankverhoudingen gaven bijna onoplosbare problemen. Toch werden de kwintetleden in de loop van dat jaar zo enthousiast dat ieder voor zich oude instrumenten begon te verzamelen. Een paar jaar lang trad het Danzi Kwintet zowel met oude als met hedendaagse instrumenten op, soms zelfs afwisselend op één concert. Naast een plaatopname van werken van Reicha, Michael Haydn en Cambini heeft dit uiteindelijk geleid tot de opnamen op authentieke instrumenten van Divertimenti en Serenades van Mozart onder leiding van Vester.

Een uitgebreide lijst van grammofoonopnamen van het Danzi Kwintet op oude en nieuwe instrumenten is te vinden onder het hoofdstuk 'Discografie'.

Onderwijs

Zonder ooit één uur stage gelopen te hebben en zonder een scriptie geschreven te hebben over 'leerinhouden en doelstellingen', heeft Frans Vester vanaf 1950 tot aan de dag van vandaag, waarop hij afscheid neemt als leraar aan het Koninklijk Conservatorium, vrijwel ononderbroken les gegeven. De stoet leerlingen die dat heeft opgeleverd is onafzienbaar. Desalniettemin tracht de aan het einde van dit artikel bijgevoegde leerlingenlijst een zo volledig mogelijk overzicht te geven van Vesters afgestudeerde leerlingen en buitenlandse gastleerlingen.

Zijn bemoeienissen met het muziekvakonderwijs begonnen in 1950, toen hij, wegens ziekte van Paul Loewer, tijdelijk diens lessen verving aan het Amsterdams Conservatorium. Behalve de leerlingen van Loewer kreeg Vester twee nieuwelingen, Rinus Winterink en Peter van Munster die, toen de vervangingsperiode voorbij was, voor elkaar kregen dat zij hun studie bij hem mochten voltooien. De voorwaarde van de directie was wel dat de lessen bij Vester thuis zouden plaatsvinden. Deze lessen in de molen 'de Slokop' bij Spaarndam waren afspiegelingen van de lessen die Vester zelf in zijn jeugd van Jos de Klerk moet hebben gehad. Ze liepen soms uit tot een hele dag gedrieën fluitspelen, onderbroken door de maaltijden die zijn vrouw Karin verzorgde.

Na een korte periode aan het Amsterdams Muzieklyceum, waar hij Johan Feltkamp, die ziek was, verving, werd Vester in 1961 in Den Haag aan het Koninklijk Conservatorium benoemd. Feltkamp, die ook in Den Haag les gaf, had daarvoor gepleit; Kees van Baaren, de directeur, stemde daar van harte mee in. Over de resultaten van zijn lessen zegt Vester zelf: 'Alleen de leerlingen met enige aanleg hebben mij overleefd', waarmee hij maar wil aangeven dat de invloed van de leraar betrekkelijk klein is. Het belangrijkste moet uit de leerling zelf komen. Vester zou Vester niet zijn als er geen controversiële aspecten aan zijn manier van lesgeven hadden gezeten. Veel van leerlingen zijn razend enthousiast, een enkeling is enthousiast razend. Zijn aversie tegen de z.g. 'internationale stijl' heeft hij uitstekend verwoord in zijn lezing voor de 'International Flute Convention' in 1980 over 'The performance of Mozart's flute music'. Zelf vleit hij zich met de gedachte leerlingen te hebben afgeleverd die niet als twee druppels water op elkaar lijken. Op het Haagse conservatorium studeerden in de loop der jaren, naast de reguliere studenten, naar schatting een dertigtal buitenlandse fluitleerlingen waaronder vooral veel Amerikanen. Aangetrokken door zijn faam, te danken aan tournees, grammofoonplaten of catalogus kwamen ze hier voor kortere of langere tijd om hun studie voort te zetten of af te maken.

Uit de wekelijkse voorspeelavonden op vrijdag, waarbij veel aandacht werd besteed aan het van

het blad lezen van stukken die vervolgens behandeld werden, ontstond later de 'repertoireklas' waarin de door Vester belangrijk geachte werken uit de fluitliteratuur werden besproken en gespeeld. Deze repetoireklas was ook toegankelijk voor studenten van de inmiddels tot de school toegetreden andere fluitleraren. Vier van hen waren oud-leerlingen, Martine Bakker, Bart Kuyken (als traversoleraar), Peter van Munster en Eric Dequeker. De andere collega's waren Mirjam Nastasi, Alex Murray, Rien de Reede en Paul Verhey.
Op verzoek van Jan van Vlijmen is Vester ook enige tijd betrokken geweest bij de schoolleiding als hoofd van de instrumentale afdeling en ensemblespel. Hij stelde o.a. de eisen op voor de UM-opleiding.

In Vesters filosofie is de conservatorium-opleiding in de eerste plaats bedoeld om een vak te leren en niet om les te leren geven. Het lesgeven zou een specialisatie moeten zijn. Zijn eigen interesse in de fluit heeft zich in de loop van de jaren steeds meer verplaatst naar muziek in het algemeen en vandaar naar bepaalde componisten. Deze gerichtheid op één bepaalde componist heeft in Den Haag een paar projecten tot gevolg gehad die zich afspeelden tussen 1980 en 1984. Vester, die het gevoel heeft dat met conservatorium-studenten bij uitstek goed valt te werken, omdat ze nog niet geïndoctrineerd of verstard zijn, voerde met leerlingen van de school Serenades en Divertimenti van Mozart en de Tafelmusik van Telemann uit. Het spreekt bijna vanzelf dat de blaaskwintetten die op het Haagse conservatorium geformeerd werden graag bij hem aanklopten en, door hem gecoached, tot opmerkelijke resultaten kwamen.
Volgens Vester is het bijbrengen van stijlgevoel een belangrijke maar tijdrovende opdracht voor iedere conservatorium-leraar. Hoe dit gerijmd zou kunnen worden met een op handen zijnde studieduurverkorting is absoluut onbegrijpelijk, vindt hij. Zeker wanneer in aanmerking wordt genomen dat fluitspelen technisch zo veel moeilijker is geworden. De componisten stellen steeds hogere eisen, steeds meer nieuwe technieken worden van de speler verlangd. Wanneer de vooropleiding tot het muziekvak kwalitatief ook steeds meer achteruit gaat doordat op het onderwijs aan de muziekscholen meer en meer wordt bezuinigd, is terugbrengen van de studieduur aan het conservatorium tot vier jaar ronduit absurd.
Dat Vester voortijdig uit het muziekvakonderwijs stapt is niet in de laatste plaats uit onvrede daarover.

Catalogus

De catalogus is het verhaal van een verzamelaar en een uit de hand gelopen verzameling. Het begint met postzegels, sigarebandjes of voetbalplaatjes. Meestal gaat het over; bij een enkeling leidt het tot iets van zulke gigantische afmetingen als 'De Vester Catalogus'.
Het begon met een klein notitieboekje waarin Vester opschreef wat aardig was om te weten of 'wat nog wel eens van pas kon komen'. Die gegevens werden gealfabetiseerd en riepen weer vragen op als 'wat heeft die componist nog meer geschreven?'. Zo ontstond bijna als vanzelf een aardig overzicht van wat er op fluitgebied bestond of ooit bestaan had. Speurtochten naar oude en nieuwe muziek brachten Vester in de jaren '56-'57 in aanraking met Richard Pringsheim van Musica Rara in Londen die daar, net als McGinnis & Marx in New York, op een zolder een exclusief muziekhandeltje dreef. Een soort luilekkerland op het gebied van antiquarische en nieuwe muziek, speciaal voor blaasinstrumenten. Pringsheim bood aan om de inmiddels tot lijvige kantoorboeken uitgegroeide gegevens over fluitmuziek als catalogus uit te geven. Zo verscheen na vijftien jaar monnikenwerk in 1967 het sindsdien over de gehele wereld bekende 'rode boek'.
De opzet van de catalogus is een vondst. Terwille van een zo groot mogelijk praktisch gebruik

maakte Vester niet alleen een indeling op naam van de componist, maar ook één naar aantal en bezetting van de instrumenten. Dit moet zeker hebben bijgedragen tot het hoge verkoopcijfer, dat Vester zelf schat op 80.000. Door middel van dit systeem heeft menig ensemble in wording zijn levensvatbaarheid, voorzover afhankelijk van het repertoire, kunnen beoordelen. De verspreiding heeft, mede door de contacten van Pringsheim achter het IJzeren Gordijn, over de hele wereld plaatsgevonden. Van Amerika, waar het onder fluitisten een best-seller is, tot Japan en zelfs tot Rusland, getuige een grammofoonplaat die Vester eens kreeg toegestuurd met daarop in het Russisch 'Bedankt voor de catalogus!'. De prijs die aanvankelijk f 17,– was, liep in de loop van de jaren op tot ca. f 35,–. Op het ogenblik worden antiquarische aanbiedingen gemeld voor f 65,–.

Hoe werd het materiaal verzameld?

Ieder boek over muziek (catalogus, biografie en dergelijke) werd nageplozen op mogelijke gegevens die van belang konden zijn. Zoals dat met verzamelen gaat kwamen soms mensen aandragen met 'ik heb er nog een paar voor je' of 'heb je die al?'. Leerlingen en collega's brachten lijsten mee uit buitenlandse bibliotheken. Zo ontstond uit diverse bronnen een overzicht van uitgegeven, onuitgegeven en ook zoekgeraakte literatuur voor de fluit, dat natuurlijk nooit compleet kan zijn maar wat volledigheid betreft zijn weerga niet heeft.

Bij het checken van het materiaal van de 18e eeuw had Vester een groot houvast aan de British Catalogue waarin alle muziek van voor 1800 die in ongeveer 200 Engelse bibliotheken aanwezig is, is opgenomen. Daar gebruikte hij later ook de 'RISM' voor, een catalogus ontstaan uit samenwerking tussen musicologen, bibliotheken en de UNESCO, waarin een overzicht wordt gegeven van wat er in bibliotheken over de hele wereld aan gedrukte muziek tot 1800 bestaat. Voor de 19e eeuw kon geput worden uit catalogi van o.a. Prill, Whistling en Hofmeister. Veel correspondentie moest worden gevoerd met bibliotheken, b.v. over daarin aanwezige manuscripten. Een tijdrovend werk omdat bibliotheken vaak weigerachtig zijn of slecht georganiseerd.

Naast de fluitmuziek gerangschikt op naam van de componist en naar bezetting, bevat de catalogus een lijst van werken voor fluit in combinatie met zangstem, een lijst van etudes en een overzicht van de in de loop der eeuwen verschenen fluitmethodes. Bovendien is een opsomming van boeken en artikelen met betrekking tot de fluit en blaasinstrumenten in het algemeen opgenomen. Aanleiding tot het samenstellen daarvan was de wens van Vester om, alvorens zelf over de fluit te schrijven, te weten wat er al eerder geschreven was. Inmiddels is de literatuur over de fluit zo uitgebreid geworden dat het een geheel eigen boek zou beslaan. Deze lijst wordt daarom niet opgenomen in de nieuwe catalogus waar Vester nu al weer jaren aan werkt en die waarschijnlijk binnen een jaar na het verschijnen van deze biografie zal worden uitgegeven. Een overzicht van fluitmethodes, die inmiddels volledig worden beschreven in Warner's *Bibliography of Woodwind Instructions Books*, komt daarin niet voor, evenmin als werken voor fluit en zang.

De opzet van de nieuwe catalogus zal anders zijn dan die van de oude. Behalve de volledige titel van een werk worden b.v. ook de bibliotheken vermeld waar het te vinden is, ongeacht of het in een moderne uitgave te krijgen is of niet. Problemen leveren werken op die anoniem zijn of die aan meerdere auteurs worden toegeschreven, zoals b.v. werken van Quantz en Frederik de Grote. Vester heeft geprobeerd deze problemen te ontraadselen. Waar dat niet mogelijk was heeft hij ze gesignaleerd en van commentaar voorzien met verwijzing naar artikelen of andere publikaties. Het eerste deel beslaat uitsluitend fluitmuziek van de 18e eeuw. Alleen al het voorwoord met veel literatuur-technische gegevens zal voor menig fluitist en onderzoeker een bron van informatie zijn.

Verzorgen van uitgaven

Wanneer men spreekt van het 'verzorgen' (tot in de puntjes en boogjes) van uitgaven, dan is dat zeker op Vester van toepassing. Niet alleen dat achter de fluitmuziek die onder zijn redactie verschijnt vaak een 'idee' zit, zoals bij de 'Classical Studies' of de 'Bach flute obbligatos', maar alle regels voor een verantwoorde uitgave worden gewetensvol toegepast en dikwijls wordt in het voorwoord zulke nuttige extra informatie gegeven dat de voorwoorden-sla-ik-over spelers het schaamrood op de kaken zouden moeten krijgen. Vesters eerste uitgaven waren Gigue-en-Rondeau en Rondeau van Michel Blavet die in 1953 bij Broekmans & Van Poppel verschenen, in 1954 gevolgd door Blavet's Concert in a. Deze stukken zijn inmiddels in herziene versie herdrukt. Bij Mills in Londen werd in 1963 'Andante en Fantasie' *für eine Orgelwalze* van Mozart, door Vester bewerkt voor blaaskwintet, uitgegeven. De bewerkingen van de Flötenuhr stukken van Haydn en Beethoven zouden daar ook verschijnen maar werden later door Universal overgenomen. Voor Musica Rara verzorgde Vester de uitgaven, in 1966, van het Quintet in f van Reicha en het Quintet in d van Danzi.

Aan de sinds 1966 bij Universal verschenen en inmiddels befaamde 'Vester etudes' ligt het idee ten grondslag om fluitleerlingen in betrekkelijk korte tijd kennis te laten maken met etudes van verschillende componisten en in verschillende stijlen, i.p.v. het laten doorwerken van dikke banden van één componist. Eerst verscheen het blauwe boek met 100, daarna het bruine met 50 'Classical studies', later, in 1976 het groene bandje met etudes op beginniveau. Gekozen werd uit verschillende periodes, van Frederik de Grote via Fürstenau en Boehm tot Gariboldi. Eveneens bij Universal verscheen de bundel met obligate fluitpartijen uit Bachcantates, bedoeld als een soort Bach-studies en als studiemateriaal voor traversospelers. Verder verzorgde Vester bij Universal nog: Drie Fantasiën van Kuhlau, voor fluit solo; Sonates voor fluit en piano en Duo's voor 2 fluiten van Mozart; Drie Andantes voor althobo en 4 blazers van Reicha (nog nooit eerder uitgegeven); Vijf Stukken voor 3 fluiten van Mozart; Duo concertant voor fluit en piano van Czerny; het Quintet no. 2 in Es van Gebauer; Twaalf Stukken 'für die Flötenuhr' van Haydn en het Concert 'in Form einer Gesangs-Szene' van Spohr.

Nieuw is Vesters idee om bundels samen te stellen met barokmuziek in verschillende nationale stijlen, Duits, Frans, Engels en Italiaans. De Duitse verzameling met werken van Telemann, Kleinknecht en Müthel wordt binnenkort door Universal op de markt gebracht.

Ook bij Broekmans & Van Poppel wordt van hem op dit moment een groot aantal nieuwe uitgaven voorbereid. In de 'Flute Series', onder redactie van Rien de Reede verschijnen binnenkort (of zijn inmiddels al verschenen) de volgende werken: Negen stukken voor één en twee fluiten van Couperin, Hotteterre en Blavet; voor twee fluiten: Drie Duetten op. 20 van Hoffmeister, Grand Duo op. 76 van Mozart en een Duo van Pleyel; voor drie fluiten: Trio op. 58 van Kummer en Trio op. 26 van Reicha; voor vier fluiten: Notturno op. 37 van De Michelis; voor fluit en b.c.: Troisième livre de sonates, deel I en II, van Blavet; voor twee fluiten en cello: bewerkingen uit Don Giovanni van Mozart.

Voor uitgeverij Knuf in Buren heeft Vester de redactie op zich genomen van 'The Flute Library'. Hierin verschenen tot nu toe:
Tromlitz - Ausführlicher und gründlicher Unterricht die Flöte zu spielen.
Tromlitz - Ueber die Flöte mit mehrern Klappen.
Hugot-Wunderlich - Méthode de Flûte.
Delusse - L'Art de la Flûte Traversière.
Corette - Méthode de la Flûte Traversière.
Ribock - Bemerkungen über die Flöte.

De Vaucanson - An Account of the Mechanism of an Automaton.
Voorhees - The classification of flute fingering systems of the nineteenth and twentieth centuries.

Publikaties

Naast de gigantische catalogus vallen de andere publikaties van Vester een beetje in het niet. Zelf zegt hij over zijn eerste en enige boekje *De Fluit*, uitgegeven in 1948 bij Lispet: 'Dat had nooit mogen gebeuren'. Toch zal in de afgelopen 35 jaar menig methodiekexamen-kandidaat er dankbaar uit hebben geput, want iets anders was en is er op dit gebied in het Nederlands niet. Door de uitgever was het oorspronkelijk bedoeld voor amateurfluitisten in b.v. harmonie-orkesten. Vester schreef het meer met het oog op staatsexamenkandidaten. In 1959 verscheen er een 'gekuiste' uitgave, d.w.z. de naar Vesters mening slechtste stukken werden er uitgehaald.
Verdere publikaties zijn: het artikel *Blazer en vibrato*, verschenen in 'Mens en Melodie', jaargang 1961 nr. 3 en 4, een paar artikelen in 'Het Parool' over Danzi en Reicha en natuurlijk de beruchte lezing die hij in 1980 hield voor de 'International Flute Convention' in Washington over *The performance of Mozart's flute music*. Het artikel *Uitgevers, bewerkers, uitgaven en Urtextedities* verschenen in 1983 in 'Fluitweek-informatie' van de IJsbreker in Amsterdam is belangrijke en onmisbare lectuur voor iedere fluitist. Het is in dit boekje opgenomen in een Engelse vertaling van David Shapero.

Nawoord

De term 'geleerd Musicus' is afkomstig van Quantz, uit de Nederlandse vertaling van diens 'Versuch'. Quantz zou Frans Vester, zo deze al geen reïncarnatie van hem is, deze titel zeker eervol verlenen. Alleen al de hierboven beschreven en nog zeer ontoereikende opsomming van Vesters activiteiten tot nu toe zouden daarvoor alle aanleiding geven. Om de vele kanten van zijn persoon te belichten zou een boek nodig zijn met de omvang van zijn eigen, binnenkort te verschijnen nieuwe catalogus. Daarin zou plaats moeten zijn voor verhalen over zijn verzamelingen oude drukken en fluiten, zijn filosofieën, zijn beurtelings zwartgallige en komische kijk op het leven, zijn wetenschappelijke benadering van alles wat met muziek te maken heeft en niet in de laatste plaats zijn weergaloos geketter en gemopper op het muziekleven in het algemeen en dat in Nederland in het bijzonder. Dat boek moet nog maar eens geschreven worden. De poging tot een biografie die ik ondernomen heb is in de eerste plaats ontstaan uit lange gesprekken met Frans Vester zelf. Aanvullende informatie kreeg ik van Arnold Swillens, Miep van Luin, Koen van Slogteren, Brian Pollard, Adriaan van Woudenberg, Desirée Lewis, Mia Dreese, Mieke Stuart, Oscar Ramspek, Anneke Uittenbosch en Veronica Hampe. Ik dank hen daarvoor hierbij hartelijk.

Discografie

Danzi Kwintet

Danzi	Quintet in Bes op. 56 no. 1
Gebauer	Quintet in Es no. 2
Mozart	Andante K 616
	Fantasie K 608
	Artone S 9508
Danzi	Quintet in g op. 56 no. 2
Haydn	7 Stücke für die Flötenuhr
Reicha	Quintet in C op. 91 no. 1
	Diskanto MAR 12901
Reicha	Quintet in G op. 88 no. 3
M. Haydn	Divertimento in D
Cambini	Quintet in F no. 3
	(op authentieke instrumenten)
	Philips 802.791 LY
Reicha	Quintet in f op. 99 no. 2
Onslow	Quintet in F op. 81
	Philips 802.792 LY
Gebauer	Quintet in Bes no. 1
Rossini	Quartet in F no. 6
Reicha	Quintet in G op. 99 no. 6
	Philips 802.869 LY
Stamitz	Quartet op. 8 no. 2
Reicha	3 Andantes
Rossini	Quartet in G no. 2
Danzi	Quintet in e op. 67 no. 2
	Philips 839.703 LY
Danzi	Quintet in d op. 68 no. 3
Haydn	7 Stücke für die Flötenuhr
Beethoven	Adagio und Allegro für die Spieluhr
Mozart	Andante K 616
	Fantasie K 608
	Seon AB 67016
Reicha	Quintet in Es op. 88 no. 2
	Quintet in d op. 88 no. 4
	Polydor Tokyo SE 7806
Danzi	3 Quintets in Bes, g en F
	Seon
Reicha	Quintet in D op. 99 no. 4
	(ook o.a. Quartet 4 fl.)
	BASF

Spohr	Quintet in c op. 52 (pf, fl, cl, fag, hn) Septet in a op. 147 (pf, vn, vc, fl, fag, hn) (met Genuit, Schröder, Bijlsma) *MPS-BASF 39 22132-6*
Hindemith	Kleine Kammermusik op. 24 no. 2 Septet (fl, ob, cl, bascl, fag, hn, trp) (met Koenen en Groot) Kanonische Sonatine op. 31 no. 3 (met Martine Bakker) *BASF Stereo 25-21639-2*
Schönberg	Quintet op. 26 *BASF Stereo 25-22057*
Schönberg Birtwhistle	Quintet op. 26 Refrains and Choruses *Philips 802.740 LY*
Stockhausen	Zeitmasse (fl, ob, eh, cl, fag) (met Holliger)
Henze	Quintet
R. Malipiero	Musica da camera
Fortner	5 Bagatellen
Becker	Serpentinata *Philips Stereo 6500 261*
Janacek	Mlâdi (fl, ob, cl, bascl, fag, hn) (met Koenen)
Krejci	Divertimento (fl, cl, trp, fag) (met Groot)
Foerster	Quintet in D op. 95 *MPS-BASF Quadrophonic SQ 25-21809-0*
Mozart	Divertimenti K 213, 253, 270, 289 (2 ob, 2 hn, 2 bn, leiding Vester) (authentieke instrumenten) *SEON*
Mozart	Serenades K 375, 388 (authentieke instrumenten, leiding Vester) *RCA RL 30342 AW*
Rheinberger	Nonet op. 139 (fl, ob, cl, fag, hn, vn, va, vc, cb) (met Schröder, Bijlsma, Peeters, Woodrow)
Lachner	Nonet in f (idem) *BASF 2921 1186-6 (2 LP.)*
Schat Ruyneman	Improvisations and Symphonies Reflexions no. 4 *Donemus DAVS 6202*
Van Baaren P. Ketting	Quintetto Trio (fl, cl, fag) *Donemus DAVS 6501*
Escher	Quintet *Donemus DAVS*

Escher	Sinfonia per dieci strumenti (met strijkkwintet van het Concertgebouworkest) *Donemus*
Van Baaren	Septet (met vn, cb) (met Schröder, Woodrow)
Van Baaren	Trio (fl, cl, fag)
Pijper	Trio (fl, cl, fag) Quintet *Donemus DAVS 7273-3*
Van Vlijmen	Quintet II *Donemus CVS 1981/3*
M. Mengelberg	Omtrent een componistenactie *Donemus CVS 1982*
De Leeuw	Antiphonie *Donemus CV 7803*
Diepenbrock	Wenn Ich ihn nur habe (sopr, fl, ob d'am, cl, fag, hn, cb) (met Elisabeth Lugt, De Gruyter) *Donemus Composer's Voice Special*
Hindemith	7 Kammermusiken (met o.a. Danzi quintet) *BASF (3 LP.) SLT 43110/12-B*

Overige opnames

Mozart	Andante in C, K 315 Concerto in C (fl/hp) K 299 (met Witsenburg) Rondo in D, K Anh 184 Concerto in D, K 314 Concerto in G, K 313 (authentieke instrumenten) (met Mozart Ensemble Amsterdam, Brüggen) *Philips 6575008/9*
Mozart	Quartet in D, K 285 (met leden van het Strauss-Quartett) *Telefunken SLT 43090-B/641009 As*
Haydn Mozart Mozart	Quartet in C Quartet in A, K 298 Quartet in C, K 285b (met Schröder, Godwin, Bijlsma) *Diskanto AKM 17443*
Telemann	Tafelmusik I Tafelmusik II Tafelmusik III (met Concerto Amsterdam, Brüggen) *Telefunken Stereo 6.35298 FX (6 LP.)*
Telemann	Concerto in e (fl, blfl) (met Brüggen, Amsterdams Kamerorkest) *Telefunken AWT 9413-C*
Telemann Fasch	Quartet in d (blfl, 2 fl, bc) Sonate in G (blfl, fl, bc)

Loeillet	Quintet in b (2 fl, 2 blfl, bc)
Quantz	Triosonate in C (blfl, fl, bc)
	(met Brüggen, Van Wingerden, Tromp, Pollard, Bijlsma, Leonhardt)
	Telefunken 6.41346 AG
Couperin	Les Nations
	(met o.a. Brüggen, Leonhardt, Bijlsma)
	Telefunken
J.S. Bach	Kantate no. 209
	(met Agnes Giebel, Leonhardt Consort)
	Telefunken SAWT 9465-B
J.S. Bach	Trauerode-Kantate
	(met Concerto Amsterdam, Leonhardt)
	Telefunken
Telemann	Quartet in A
C.Ph.E. Bach	Triosonate in d Wotq. 145
J.S. Bach	Triosonate in c (Musikalisches Opfer)
	(Estro Armonico op authentieke instrumenten)
	MPS 13003 ST
Frederik de Grote	Sonate in d
	(met Leonhardt, Bijlsma)
	Telefunken SMT 1307
J.S. Bach	Sonates in e, G, E, b
	(met Bakker, Uittenbosch, Van Ast)
	Diskanto AKM 17449
F.H. Graf	Quartet in G no. 2
	Quartet in C no. 3
	(met Schröder, Peeters, Bijlsma)
	BASF KBF-21195
Amon	Quartet in D op. 85
	(met R. Kussmaul, J. Kussmaul, Bijlsma)
	BASF KBF-21189
Fröhlich	Serenade (fl, cl, va, vc)
	(met Klöcker, Kussmaul, Bijlsma)
	MPS-BASF 329 1986-0
F. Benda	Concerto in e
Haydn	Concerto in D
Gluck	Reigen seliger Geister
	(met Concerto Amsterdam)
	BASF KBF-20838
Haydn	Concerto in D
Telemann	Concerto in D
Pergolesi	Concerto in G
	Diskanto SP 65010
Pokorny	Concerto in D
	(met Concerto Amsterdam, Schröder)
	BASF KBF 21.191
Mahaut	Concerto in e
	(met Nederlands Kamerorkest)
	Donemus DAVS

Haydn	5 Stücke für die Flötenuhr (met Miep van Luin) *Columbia 78 t.*
Schubert	Variaties op. 160 (met Genuit) Quartet (fl, va, vc, guit) (met Kussmaul, Bijlsma, Goudswaard) *MPS-BASF 39 21811 (2 LP.)*
Kuhlau	Sonate in a op. 85 Duo in g op. 87 no. 2 Divertissement op. 68 no. 5 (met Genuit, Bakker) *Polydor, Tokyo SE 7803*
Beethoven	Allegro und Menuett (authentieke instrumenten met Bakker) *Telefunken SAWT 9547-A*
Czerny	Fantasie (fl, vc, pf) (met Bijlsma, Hoogland) *BASF*
C.M. von Weber	Trio in g op. 63 (met Bijlsma, Hoogland) 10 Melodies of Scotland (met Van Egmond, Partridge, Watkinson, Beths, Bijlsma, Hoogland) *Edition MP 60.30010*
Debussy	Syrinx Sonate (fl, va, hp) (met Schröder, Witsenburg) *Acanta EA 21.814 Stereo*
Castiglioni	Gymel (met Bruins) *Philips*
Kreutzer	Quintet (fl, cl, va, vc, pf) (met Consortium Classicum) *MPS/BASF*
Von Winter	Octet (met Consortium Classicum) *MPS/BASF*
Nisle	Septet (met Consortium Classicum) *MPS/BASF*
Fr. Martin	Lieder (met Van Egmond, Schröder, Bijlsma) *BASF*

Leerlingenlijst

1954 Peter van Munster	1971 Bart Kuyken	**gastleerlingen:**
Rinus Winterink	Lien v.d. Poel	
1961 Judith Dresden	Brigitte Woudenberg	Ronald van den Berghe
Nanda Hoogeveen	1972 Margriet Evers	Jane Bowers
Lucius Voorhorst	Ferenc Hutyra	Jorge Caryevschi
1963 Govert Jurriaanse	1973 Wim Steinman	Patrick Deygers
1964 Linda Möhringer	Yke Toepoel	Greer Ellison
Peter Quakernaat	Froukje Wiebenga	Judy Fisher
Mieke Stuart	1974 Eric Dequeker	Andrew Gerzso
1965 Lens Derogée	Monique Laanen	Clifford Goldstrom
Alain Winkelman	Vivienne Pasman	Yudianto Hinupuwadi
1966 Theo Boekkooi	Maaike de Rijk	Claude Hutter
1967 Dick Hoogeveen	1975 John Bhaggan	Frieda Jacobowitz
Alfons van Leggelo	Joosje Everwijn	Linny Kammer
1968 Jan van den Berg	Anneke van Gessel	Kathleen Kraft
David Porcelijn	G. Savelkoel	Kunimitsu Morimoto
Barend Schuurman	1976 Roger Roselle	Llorenc Caballero Pamies
1969 Chris Hinze	1979 Wouter v.d. Berg	Nancy Possman
1970 Marga van Bree	Greer Ellison	Catherine Saunders
Mia Dreese	Judah Engelsberg	Janet See
Elly Groen	Pieter Prick	Helmut Stocker
Renee Hesmerg	Stephen Schulz	Joanna Turska
Alfons Tel	1980 Donna Metz	Natalia Valderrama Rouy
Arianne Veelo	1981 Marten Root	Maurice Verstuyft
	Marieke Schneemann	Courtny Westcott
	1982 Berdien Steunenberg	
	1983 Marion Moonen	
	Kathinka Pasveer	
	Evelien Poser	
	Dorien Schade	
	Hans Wolff	
	1984 Hanneke Provily	
	Jolanda Romkes	

Frans Vester - A 'learned musician' *

Peter van Munster

Education

Frans Vester was born on May 22, 1922 in The Hague and moved to Beverwijk with his parents and sister at the age of seven. His father, an amateur violinist, encouraged the boy's interest in music, which was initially directed towards the piano. Vester first became interested in the flute after reading a children's book about a boy who played the recorder in order to forget his home-sickness.

Vester's first teacher was Jos de Klerk, a musician and music critic in Haarlem. He was of great importance to Vester's musical development. From his 11th year on Vester received from him not only flute lessons, but was also instructed in harmony, sight reading, music theory and orchestration. In 1937, after four years of study with De Klerk, the 15-year-old Vester began his studies at the Amsterdam Conservatory. There he studied with Hubert Barwahser, at that time the first flutist of the Concertgebouw Orchestra. During his years at the conservatory Vester's interest in the flute weakened, only to be revived upon hearing recordings of the French flutist Marcel Moyse. From that time on, his development was greatly influenced by the French school of flute playing.

During the war, Vester enrolled as a composition student at the Royal Conservatory in The Hague to avoid being sent to work in Germany. There he studied for a short time with Henk Badings and composed several works. These works, which include an oboe concerto and pieces for trumpet and piano, have been performed in The Netherlands, but he himself considers them to be of little worth.

Orchestras

In 1941 Vester became second flutist of one of the oldest orchestras in The Netherlands, The Haarlem Orchestra (De Haarlemse Orkest Vereniging). After the war Vester was employed by The Netherlands Broadcasting Foundation (De Nederlandse Radio Unie), first with The Radio Chamber Orchestra (Het Radio Kamerorkest) and later with The Promenade Orchestra (Het Promenade Orkest). He had many opportunities there to perform as a soloist. His repertoire included the concerti of Mozart, Pendleton, Nielsen and Ibert.

From 1955 until 1966, Vester occupied the first chair of The Netherlands Opera (De Nederlandse Opera) in Amsterdam. In addition to the opera orchestra, he was for two years the flutist of The Netherlands Chamber Orchestra (Het Nederlands Kamerorkest), an ensemble originally organized to perform at the annual Holland Festival and to promote The Netherlands by means of tours abroad.

*After Quantz.

Danzi Quintet

Chamber Music

Vester's greatest love lies in the study and playing of chamber music. His experience ranges from a flute and piano duo to an ensemble of nine players, in styles encompassing music of the 18th century to the present.

His first long-lasting musical association was with pianist Miep van Luin. As a duo they performed together for approximately fifteen years, touring primarily in the Benelux countries with a repertoire hosting standard works as well as newer literature, such as the Sonatine by Boulez. In 1953 Vester formed Arte Fiato with radio colleagues Koen van Slogteren (oboe) and Arnold Swillens (bassoon). They were later joined by Hans Brandts Buys (harpsichord). For the next six years this ensemble appeared regularly at home and abroad.

In 1956 Vester formed the Danzi Quintet with Brian Pollard (bassoon), Adriaan van Woudenberg (french horn), Koen van Slogteren (oboe) and Pem Godrie (clarinet). Following the departure of Van Slogteren, twelve years later, Maarten Karres, Han de Vries and Jan Spronk, successively, served as oboist. Piet Honingh succeeded Godrie as clarinettist after six years and remained with the group until it was disbanded in 1978.

The quintet was originally founded to realize Vester's desire to perform the Wind Quintet, op. 26 by Arnold Schönberg. After more than a year of intensive rehearsals their debut was made at the Holland Festival in the summer of 1958. The ensemble was immediately successful and received much critical acclaim abroad during tours in Europe, the Middle-East, The Soviet Union and The United States.

During its long tenure the quintet's repertoire ranged from 18th-century music played on original instruments, to contemporary works written specifically for them by such influential Dutch composers as: Ton de Leeuw, Peter Schat, Kees van Baaren, Rudolf Escher and Jan van Vlijmen. The Danzi Quintet has made many recordings; for a discography see page 23.

While in The Netherlands Chamber Orchestra Vester and acquaintances such as Anner Bijlsma (cello), Gustav Leonhardt (harpsichord), Frans Brüggen (recorder) and Jaap Schröder (violin) began a search for a performance style of 18th- and 19th-century music. Their dissatisfaction with the performing of this music in late-Romantic style led to a thorough study of 18th- and 19th-century sources. This approach to the performance of historical music has had far-reaching effects both in The Netherlands and abroad.

Vester's interest in the baroque flute in the 1950's led to the making of recordings such as the complete Mozart flute concerti with the Mozart Ensemble Amsterdam, conducted by Frans Brüggen, and performed on historical instruments. In 1967 a new ensemble with Jaap Schröder (baroque violin), Veronica Hampe (viola da gamba) and Anneke Uittenbosch (harpsichord) was formed: Estro Armonico Amsterdam. Vester currently plays in the Harmonicon Ensemble, established in 1980 to perform large-scale classical and romantic works of varying instrumentation, such as the Hummel Septet and the Spohr Nonet.

Teaching

Vester has been involved with music education in The Netherlands since 1950; initially for some years as a flute teacher at the Amsterdam Conservatory and afterwards from 1961 to 1984 as a professor of flute and chamber music at the Royal Conservatory in The Hague. Many flutists have come from abroad in the course of the years to study with Vester. For a summary of Vester's graduated pupils and guest students, see page 28.

Editing and Publications

Vester's first editorial work was undertaken in 1953 for Broekmans & Van Poppel. These editions of Michel Blavet's *Gigue-en-Rondeau* and *Rondeau* have now been re-issued. His editorial work continued and broadened in scope with his transcriptions for wind quintet of Mozart's *Andante, KV. 616*, and *Fantasie für eine Orgelwalze, KV. 608*, for Mills of London in 1963. Work for Musica Rara followed with the publication of Danzi and Reicha quintets in 1966. Vester has also compiled a three-volume series of progressive studies entitled 'Classical Studies' for Universal Edition. Over the years he has edited for Universal such works as Czerny's *Duo Concertante*, op. 129 for flute and piano, *Three Fantasias* for solo flute by F. Kuhlau, and *Six Duets* for two flutes by W.A. Mozart. He is currently compiling four collections of French, German, English and Spanish baroque music. His fruitful association with Broekmans & Van Poppel has resulted in the publishing of Blavet's *Troisième livre de sonates pour la flûte traversière avec la basse* (Vols. 1 and 2) with figured bass realization by Anneke Uittenbosch; *Recueil de pièces*, nine pieces for one and two flutes by F. Couperin, J. Hotteterre and M. Blavet; and *Don Giovanni* (from an edition of 1818) by W.A. Mozart for flute, violin and cello, as well as various other works.

In an effort to make important historical information on flute-playing more readily available to the serious student of music Vester has edited a series for F. Knuf (Buren) entitled 'The Flute Library' in which old flute methods and treatises, such as: J. de Vaucanson, *Le Mécanisme du Fluteur Automate...* (Paris, 1738) / *An Account of the Mechanism of an Automaton or Image playing on the German Flute...* (London, 1742); Charles Delusse, *L'Art de la Flûte traversière* (Paris, 1760); M. Corrette, *Methode pour apprendre aisément à jouer de la flûte traversière* (Paris, 1735); J.G. Tromlitz, *Ausführlicher und gründlicher Unterricht die Flöte zu spielen* (Leipzig, 1791); A. Hugot & J.G. Wunderlich, *Méthode de Flûte* (Paris, 1804); and others are published.

The *Flute Repertoire Catalogue*, published by Musica Rara in 1967 is one of his most important undertakings. To this date more than 80,000 copies have been sold throughout the world. His new revised edition, beginning with an expanded catalogue over music of the 18th century, includes complete titles from all listed works, libraries where the autographs or manuscripts are located, and detailed commentary and reference information for pieces of questionable origin, authorship and instrumentation.

Other publications by Vester include a booklet *De Fluit* (The Flute) written in 1948; an article *Blazer en Vibrato* (Wind Player and Vibrato) printed in 'Mens en Melodie' 1961/3 and 4; an article *On the Performance of Mozart's Flute Music* which appeared in the Newsletter of the National Flute Association, Vol. VI, no. 1 (Fall 1980), being the printed version of a lecture given in 1980 at the Convention of the National Flute Association in Washington D.C.; and an article *Uitgevers, Bewerkers, Uitgaven en Urtextedities*, which appeared in 1983 in Fluitweek Informatie (a program regarding the Flute Week, a week-long course held annually in Amsterdam), published in this book in an English translation by David Shapero under the title *Publishers, Editors, Editions and Urtexts*.

Translation: Frieda Leia Jacobowitz

The Hotteterre family of woodwind instrument makers

Jane M. Bowers

The Hotteterre family is sometimes credited with initiating extremely important changes that took place in the construction of woodwind instruments during the second half of the seventeenth century - the development of the oboe from the shawm, the bassoon from the curtal, the conical one-keyed transverse flute from the cylindrical flute, and the three-jointed recorder from that of one piece.[1] Although their leadership in this area cannot be proved and certainly should not be unequivocally asserted, the importance of their work was acknowledged by their contemporaries. Michel de La Barre attributed the transformation of the oboe into an instrument 'suitable for concerts' to the Hotteterres and Philidors.[2] Pierre Borjon de Scellery, in his *Traité de la musette* of 1672, wrote:

Those that have become the most esteemed in this kingdom through their composition and their playing, and through their skill in making musettes, are the Hotteterres. The father is a man unique for the construction of all kinds of instruments of wood, of ivory, and of ebony, such as musettes, flûtes,* flageolets, oboes and cromornes, and even for making complete families of all these instruments. His sons are in no way inferior to him in the practice of this art, with which they have combined a complete understanding, and a still more admirable mastery of the playing of the musette in particular.[3]

In his *Livre commode des adresses de Paris pour 1692*, Abraham du Pradel cited three of the Hotteterres - Colin (Nicolas [III]), Jean (III), and Louis (V) - for excellence in making and playing wind instruments.[4] The principal known makers are Jean (I) (?-1690/92?), Nicolas (II) (*l'aîné*) (c1637-1694), Louis (V) (?-1716), Nicolas (III) (*le jeune* or Colin) (1653-1727), Jean (III) (c1648-1732), Martin (?-1712), and Jacques ('le Romain') (1674-1763). Others, about whom little is known, are Nicolas (I) (?-1693),[5] Louis (IV) (?-1692),[6] Philippe (I) (1681-1763),[7] Philippe (II) (1714-1773),[8] and Louis (VI) (1717-1801).[9] (See the accompanying family tree.) The extent of past confusion surrounding the activities of the various instrument makers in the family, however, suggests that a discussion reflecting the current state of knowledge about all its most important craftsmen might be useful in helping clarify the contributions each might have made to the rapidly developing art of woodwind instrument building.

---

* Readers should be warned that the term *flûte* (and its plural) in seventeenth- and early eighteenth-century French sources usually did not refer to the transverse flute (which more frequently was indicated by such terms as *flûte d'Allemagne* and *flûte traversière*); rather, it customarily referred either to what we now call the recorder or, especially after the rise in fashionability of the one-keyed transverse flute in the last decade of the seventeenth century, to both types of instruments together. Rather than impose on the reader my own interpretation of the term *flûte* in each source I quote, I shall give it precisely as it appears without translation. With regard to this passage in the Borjon treatise, however, let me suggest that the term *flûtes* probably referred only to recorders, since transverse flutes were rarely made and played around the date of publication of this treatise; the flute's transformation and revival occurred a little later.

Jean (I)

The founder of the Hotteterre family of instrument makers seems to have been Loys de Haulteterre (*d* by 1628), who worked as a wood turner ('tourneur en boys') in the district of La Couture-Boussey in Normandy during the early seventeenth century. He and his wife Jehanne Gabriel are known to have had eight children, several of whom emigrated to Paris where they established themselves as musicians and instrument makers. Jean (I) (?-1690/92?) was probably the first to do so. He was already a master wood turner ('maistre tourneur en boys') in the town of La Couture at the time of his marriage to Marguerite Delalande in 1628 (signing his name 'Jehan Hauterre' on the marriage contract, although in all later signatures he spelled his last name 'Hoteterre'). By 1636 he had settled in Paris.[10] He is probably the Jehan Hotteterre who was described as a 'master player of instruments' in the records of a baptism at which he was godfather in 1640 as well as the one described as a 'master maker of instruments' in the records of the baptism of his son Hilaire on 22 October 1646.[11] In 1648 he was listed as a 'master maker of instruments' when he signed as a witness at the wedding of Abraham Dufour and Françoise Du Bault,[12] and in 1656, as 'musette du roi' when he witnessed the wedding of Jean Brunet and Catherine de Bonière.[13] In the same year, Michel de Marolles cited the ravishing flageolet playing of one of the Hotteterres: '... and many have been ravished by the kit ('poche') and the violin of Constantin and Bocan; by the viol of Otman and Mogar, by the musette of Poitevin, by the recorder ('flûte douce') of La Pierre and by the flageolet of Osteterre'.[14] Since Jean (I) was the longest established of any of his family in Paris, it was probably to his playing that Marolles referred.

Already around 1650 Jean (I) had been admitted to the Hautbois et Musettes du Poitou, in which he served as 'dessus' until being replaced by his son Martin in 1667.[15] In 1657 various members of the Hotteterre family began to be listed in the librettos of the ballets danced at court, though they were not mentioned by first name. Jean (I) seems to have been the one referred to as 'Obterre le pere' in some of the librettos and among the 'quatres Opterre' listed in others.[16] It seems indisputable that he was also the 'father' of the Hotteterres who, according to Borjon, excelled in making all kinds of wind instruments, since aside from his brother Nicolas (I) (*d* 1693), whose abilities as a maker are somewhat questionable (see below), he was the only family member of his generation to have been clearly active as a maker. From Borjon we learn that Jean (I) made not only musettes but also *flûtes*, flageolets, oboes and *cromornes*. His activities with regard to the musette are also mentioned by his grandson Jacques Hotteterre, who wrote that Jean (I) had perfected the drones ('bourdons') of that instrument, without specifying precisely how.[17]

In spite of his obvious success in Paris, Jean (I) remained attached to the region of his birth; he began buying property there in 1657, and he was to return to the region later, although the date when he left Paris is unclear. On 16 April 1664 he seems to have bought a house at La Couture,[18] and on the very next day, the minutes of Anet record that 'noble homme Jean de Hauteterre, bourgeois de Paris, l'un des quatre hautbois et joueur de musette du Roy' bought a house in the town of Evreux, where the sign L'ANCRE NOIRE hung.[19] Even before this latter document was found, Ernest Thoinan suggested in his seminal study of the family that the sign of the anchor, which appears on a number of instruments marked HOTTETERRE, might have been Jean (I)'s sign which was inherited first by his son Martin and then by his grandson Jacques.[20] But we do not know whether Jean ever lived in the house with the sign of the anchor, and if he did, how long he remained there. In 1671 he rented houses in La Couture and Buissons to Pierre

Cousturier, and in the house at La Couture he reserved for himself several rooms and a shop. In a legal transaction dated 27 July 1681 he was said to be living in Paris, but he also reserved the house in Buissons for himself. In 1689 while living at Buissons, he bought another house in La Couture and shortly after that disappeared from view. Nicolas Mauger thinks that he probably died between 1690 and 1692, when the registers of the *état civil* of La Couture are missing.[21]

Nicolas (II)

After Jean (I), the next member of the Hotteterre family to emigrate to Paris was probably Jean's nephew Nicolas (II) (c1637-1694). Born in La Couture to Nicolas (I) (?-1693) and Anne Mauger around 1637,[22] Nicolas (II) went to Paris as a young man. In 1657 'Les Sieurs Obterre le père, Obterre fils aisné, [and] Obterre le cadet' were among the musicians who played in the 'Concert champestre de l'Espoux' in *L'Amour malade*,[23] and since Jean (I) seems to have had only one son who reached maturity (Martin), it may be that he passed off his newly arrived nephew from the country as one of his sons. In any case, Nicolas's participation as a player of the oboe, *flûte*, and musette in the *Ballets du roi* is confirmed by the appearance of his first name in the librettos in 1660.[24] By 1666 he had become 'dessus de hautbois et haute contre de violon' in the Grands Hautbois, in which his uncle Jean (II) (*le jeune*), his cousin Martin, and his brother Louis (V) were also listed as members for the first time that year (the documents from 1665 are missing).[25] By the late 1650s he must already have established himself in Paris as an instrument maker and teacher, and by 1660 he had sent for his father and begun working with him in instrument making (see the declaration of Anne Mauger quoted below; another document indicates that the father and son were living together on the rue des Arcis in 1660).[26] Later, however, Nicolas (II) struck out on his own, leaving his brothers Louis (V) and later Nicolas (III) (Colin) to work with their father.

In 1675 Nicolas (I) made a deed of gift to his four sons - Nicolas (II), Louis (V), Nicolas (III) and Jean (IV), which after the death of Jean in 1683 was confirmed on behalf of the first three.[27] An inventory made after the elder Nicolas's death in 1693 became the departure for a law suit among the heirs, in consequence of which Nicolas's widow, Anne Mauger, made a declaration which reveals some important information about the family:

19 September 1693, at Ivry, before the notaries... Anne Mauger, widow of Nicolas Hauteterre, while living a citizen of Paris, in order to establish peace in the family and contribute to annulling the lawsuits that exist among her children..., being obliged for the relief of her conscience to say the truth..., has by these presents declared that the goods that they had acquired proceeded as much from the work of their children as from their father.
That, in the first place, Nicolas, their oldest brother, who was in Paris before their father, earned his living by making musical instruments and teaching how to play them....
He had his father come to live with him in Paris, and then the aforesaid person appearing in court [Anne Mauger], where, having worked together with their son, they determined to marry Anne their daughter, presently wife of M. Claude Coricon, and they would have given her in marriage more than their other children might have expected, which they did with the idea that they would come by other goods....
As in effect, Nicolas their oldest son having worked a few years and having left his father, Louis, their second son, took his place and then Nicolas, their third son, and that aforesaid Mauger received all the money, as much from the earnings of the work of their children proceeding from the opéra and écoliers that they taught as from the instruments that they sold,

which were perfected by them, being certain that the deceased their father did not know how to render them in tune, as is well known to all those who knew him; so that the same money that was used to acquire the goods proceeded from the work and industry of the aforesaid Nicolas, Louis and Nicolas, their children, and that the deceased and the aforesaid Mauger did not believe that they could in good conscience dispense with making the deeds of gift that they made to them, which ought not be based on what they had given their daughter, since, in fairness, she received much more than she could have hoped for of the aforesaid goods, which the aforesaid Mauger has declared, in her soul and conscience, before us, the above-named notaries and witnesses, to be true, concerning which she has had this act drawn up to serve and to benefit her aforesaid children, in such time and place as might be necessary. Made and passed, etc.[28]

Here is the evidence that Nicolas (II) was the first of his family to go to Paris and that he was already making instruments and teaching there at the time he sent for his father. Here too is evidence that Nicolas (I) was not as skilled an instrument maker as his sons, since he could not render the instruments in tune, and that this was a well-known fact. In spite of this, Nicolas (I) may have continued to work on his own after all his sons had left home (which we know from the different addresses at which they lived at later dates), since an inventory made after his decease reveals some tools serving in his trade, some musette pieces, and some reed with which to make reeds.[29]

As for Nicolas (II), a document of 13 July 1682 touching on an advance of 1200 *livres* he made to Jérôme Noblet indicates that he was then living in Versailles, and in 1685 he received a licence to build a house there on the Place de Bourgogne. It was in Versailles that he died on 10 May 1694, apparently having continued to serve in the Grands Hautbois up until the time of his death.[30] An inventory made after his decease at the request of his widow, Marguerite de Baune, listed some 'iron tools serving to make wind instruments, such as *flûtes*, flageolets, bassoons',[31] but it is not clear whether the instrument-making appurtenances were numerous enough to constitute an active workshop. The same is true for Nicolas (I). Thus the lengths of their working periods as instrument builders are unknown.

In addition to his other activities, Nicolas (II) may have given some time to composing, or at least to arranging, for Fétis claimed to have owned an autograph manuscript *Recueil de bransles, petits ballets, courantes de cour et de ville et autres hautes et basses danses pour six parties à jouer sur les dessus et basses de violon et hautbois* of his; if so, it disappeared long ago.[32]

Louis (V)

Louis (V) (?-1716), the second son in the family of Nicolas (I), must have moved with his family to Paris at the time Nicolas (II) brought his father there. According to Thoinan, he was working as a musician at court by 1664 when he played the *flûte* in the *Plaisirs de l'Ile enchantée*, and his name appears frequently in the librettos of court productions as a *flûte* and oboe player.[33] In 1665 he entered the Grands Hautbois as 'saqueboute et taille de violon', retaining that post for the rest of his life, although he gave the reversion of his place in 1714 to his grandnephew Pierre Chédeville.[34] From the declaration quoted above, we know that he began making instruments in the family workshop. Later he too established his own workshop and acquired sufficient renown to be cited by Du Pradel in the supplement to his *Livre commode ... pour 1692* as 'Louis Horteterre [sic], near Saint Jacques de la Boucherie, for all the wind instruments.'[35] In the 1690s he seems to have begun acquiring property in La Couture and Ivry, and after the death of his mother in August 1700 he inherited several houses in and around Ivry la Chausée, which he sold to Nicolas Mercier de Villeneuve in 1709.[36] He may still have been living in Paris in 1710, but by 1714 he had moved to Ivry, and he died there in August 1716;[37] later appearances of his name on wage lists are erroneous.

Nicolas (III)

The third son in the family of Nicolas (I) to become an instrument maker was Nicolas (III) (*le jeune* or *le cadet*) (1653-1727), also sometimes referred to as Colin. Baptised on 19 February 1653 in La Couture,[38] Nicolas (III) must still have been very young when the family moved to Paris. Probably in 1666 he entered the Grands Hautbois as 'haute contre de hautbois et haute contre de violon', taking over the post from his cousin Martin and retaining it until his death on 14 December 1727.[39] From the time he entered the Grands Hautbois, he also took part alongside the other Hotteterres in all the solemnities celebrated at court, according to Thoinan. In 1672 he was oboist in the first and second companies of the *Mousquetaires du roi*. Later, around 1713, he played in the *grand choeur* of the orchestra of the Opéra.[40]

On 20 August 1685 Nicolas (III) and Catherine Chevalier, the daughter of a lawyer in Ivry, François Chevalier, signed a contract of marriage, and around 1694 a daughter, Catherine, was born to them.[41] In the same year, Nicolas began to accumulate real estate in astonishing quantities. This included houses and land in Gentilly, Ivry, Serez (a noble fief, acquired in 1705), Boussey, La Couture, Vaugirard, and other places, most of which were leased or rented out.[42] After his wife died on 13 March 1708, Nicolas requested that an inventory be made of their goods, and something of their well-to-do financial condition as well as their wide-ranging intellectual interests can be seen from some of the items listed therein: an ebony clock decorated with brass plates made in Paris by Champion, a silver watch *à reveille* with silver chain made in Rennes by Leconte, a gold enameled ring mounted with diamonds, and an astonishing library especially rich in history and literature (both ancient and modern), which also included works on religious subjects, the operas of Lully, and other music. Among the items that attest to Nicolas (III)'s profession as an instrument maker were numerous tools used for making instruments, over 900 pieces of wood in various stages of preparation, pieces of ivory and brass, reeds of various sorts, and 32 oboes, *fluttes*, and other unfinished instruments. For the use of Nicolas himself, there was one oboe and one *flutte*.[43]

As a maker Nicolas (III) must have gained considerable renown, for he was cited in Du Pradel's *Livre commode* of 1692 as one of the 'masters for the playing and fabrication of wind instruments, *flûtes*, flageolets, oboes, bassoons, musettes, etc.'[44] His working period was a long one, for he seems to have begun making instruments in the late 1650s and continued right up to the time of his death in 1727; an inventory made after his decease lists numerous tools and materials used to make *flutes traversieres ou allemandes, hautbois* [sic] *et autres instrumens*, thirty-six unfinished oboes, another two dozen unfinished *fluttes* and oboes, two musettes — one made of ivory and decorated with silver and the other made of plum wood, and two bassoons. Other items included clocks, tapestries, paintings, mirrors, a great deal of silver, and an even more extensive library than that catalogued after Nicolas's wife's death.[45] Though his will of 13 or 30 May 1718 made his niece Anne Coricon (the widow of Pierre Chédeville and the mother of the instrumentalists, instrument makers, and composers Pierre, Esprit-Philippe, and Nicolas Chédeville) his residuary legatee, he also made generous gifts to other relatives and friends as well as to his servant Jacquelon.[46] But the extent of his fortune seems to have led others to contest his will, and after his death his nieces Anne Coricon, Barbe Coricon (the widow of Jacques Deshayes), and Marie-Madeleine Hotteterre (the widow of Pierre Brechon), presented themselves as his heirs, each for a third of their uncle's estate, while in addition, Jean-Noël Marchand, the son of his deceased niece Marie-Marguerite Hotteterre, presented himself as an heir for a fourth of the property situated in the *Coutume* of Normandy. Later, on 2 July 1728, Anne Coricon renounced the residuary legacy left her by her uncle.[47]

Jean (III)

With the death of Nicolas (III), the first generation of the family of Nicolas (I) came to an end. While the next generation, primarily comprised of women, did not produce any known instrument makers, in the following one that activity was again pursued by Esprit-Philippe and Nicolas Chédeville, grandnephews of Nicolas (III), who became well known as musette makers.[48]

During the same period during which the brothers Nicolas (II), Louis (V), and Nicolas (III) were working, however, two of their cousins, Jean (III) (c 1648-1732) and Martin (?-1712), were also active and renowned as instrument makers. Jean (III) was born to Marie Mauger and Louis (I) — possibly the oldest brother in the generation that had produced Jean (I) and Nicolas (I) — in La Couture around 1648,[49] and he remained in the country until after his father died, which occurred a little before 1671, according to Thoinan. By 1676 he was in Paris, for on 10 January he took part, playing the oboe and *flûte*, in a performance of *Atys* presented at Saint Germain. He also played the *flûte*, as one of four satyrs, alongside Louis, Jean, and Nicolas Hotteterre in a performance of *Isis* at Saint Germain during Carnival in 1677.[50] On 25 May 1683 he took over the place of his deceased cousin Jean (IV) as 'basse de hautbois et taille de violon' in the Grands Hautbois.[51] His tenure in that organization was a long one, for only in 1723 did he pass the reversion of his charge to Esprit-Philippe Chédeville, which in 1725 he further transferred to Esprit-Philippe's younger brother Nicolas, since Esprit-Philippe took over another brother Pierre's post in the Grands Hautbois when Pierre died on 24 September of that year. Although Jean (III)'s name continued to be listed in the Grands Hautbois through 1731, it seems that his resignation actually occured in 1725, since a document dated 20 October 1725 says that a charge in the Grands Hautbois, 'vacant through the resignation of Jean Hotteterre', was acquired by Nicolas Chédeville.[52]

Jean's principal occupation, however, seems to have been that of instrument maker, and he was known as one of the best in Paris. In 1692 Du Pradel listed him, then living on the rue des Fossés-Saint-Germain, as one of the 'masters for the playing and fabrication of wind instruments...', and in 1701 Joseph Sauveur stated that he and Jean-Jacques Rippert were among the 'most capable makers of Paris' for woodwind instruments.[53] By 1718, when Nicolas (III) made out his will leaving Jean a pension for life of 200 *livres* to begin on the day of Nicolas's death, Jean had moved to the rue de la Harpe.[54] Just how long he was active as a maker is uncertain. While the possessions catalogued after his death included a turning wheel, an ebony bench, and some 100 tools for turning, the remaining appurtenances of his trade, when compared to those left after the death of Nicolas (III), suggest that Jean (III) did not remain as active as Nicolas during the last years of his life.

The details of Jean (III)'s death are better known than those of any of the other Hotteterres, for on Wednesday morning, 20 February 1732, Jacques Hotteterre and Esprit-Philippe and Nicolas Chédeville reported to the civil authorities that 'their cousin', Jean, eighty-four years old, living on the rue de la Harpe, had been missing since Monday evening; none of his cousins had seen him and his door had remained closed although they had knocked violently many times. A commissioner was designated to accompany them, and when they had gained access to Jean's rooms, they found the body of the old musician, 'stretched out in his bed, covered with his blanket and his clothes'. Death was said to have been caused by apoplexy since the body had no wounds or injuries. The interment took place the same day at Saint-Severin. An inventory made of the deceased's goods included, in addition to the items mentioned above, an ivory musette with an ebony bourdon, several *vieilles flûtes*, household goods, furniture, clothing, wigs, a sword, an old Grands Hautbois costume decorated with silver, eight paintings including two of the Lord and the Virgin, the portrait of the deceased (of which all trace has been lost), twenty books, mainly devotional in nature, and 1633 *livres*. Jean (III) seems never to have married or to have had children; his heirs were the children of his brothers Louis (III) and (IV) — Philippe (I), Catherine (the wife of Guillaume Angibaut), and Marguerite (the widow of Jacques Chevard).[55]

Martin

Martin, the only remaining member of the generation of Hotteterres that included Jean (III) and the brothers Nicolas, Louis, and Nicolas, to distinguish himself as an instrument maker, is the only known surviving descendant of the famous Jean (I) — the latter's son Hilaire baptised in 1646 (see p. 34 above) apparently having died young, since no further traces of him can be found. Though the date of Martin's birth is not known, it may be that it occurred in the early 1640s, since it is likely that Martin was one of the Hotteterres who played in *L'Amour malade* in 1657 (see p. 35 above), and his name is mentioned at a performance of Cavalli's *Xerse* given in 1660 for the celebrations of the marriage of Louis XIV and Maria Theresia. From this time on, according to Thoinan, Martin took part in all the celebrations at court alongside his relatives, the Piesches, Philbert, and the two Descoteauxes, playing the *flûte*, oboe, and musette.[56]

The first of the royal musical organizations in which Martin obtained a post was that of the Grands Hautbois; in 1665 or 1666 he replaced Martin Toussaint as 'haute contre de hautbois et haute contre de violon' in that organization. In 1667, however, he replaced his father in the Hautbois et Musettes du Poitou, and the Grands Hautbois post went to Nicolas (III). He was living at this time 'à la petite porte du palais, à la musette' (at the little entrance to the palace, at the sign of the musette). Though he appears to have continued playing in the Hautbois et Musettes up until the time of his death, he may have shared the post with his son Jean (V) after he obtained its reversion for him in 1699.[57]

As we have already seen, Borjon credited the sons of Jean (I) with particular skill in making all kinds of woodwind instruments, including musettes, as well as with 'a still more admirable mastery of the playing of the musette in particular'. Since Martin seems to have been Jean's only surviving son, he certainly must have been among the younger Hotteterres to whom Borjon referred. And Borjon went on to describe improvements in the instrument that one of the Hotteterres had effected:

The simple chanter can only play a tenth or twelfth, depending on the keys that are put on it; but now that le sieur Hotteterre has added a second, called the little chanter ['le petit chalumeau'], one can say that he has perfected the musette as much as one could desire, since on it one can now play the sharps and flats that lend all the beauty and precision to the airs that one plays; and by means of this little chanter one can ascend by tones, semitones, sharps and flats, up to nineteen and twenty degrees consecutively ...

What is admirable in the invention of these keys, is that the fingers for which they are made are not occupied on the simple and ordinary chanters, and in this the good sense of the inventor of this little chanter has appeared; because in order to add to the musette that which it lacked, he has found a way to occupy two fingers, that is the little finger of the left hand and the thumb of the right, that were not [formerly] used. And to speak the truth, the beauty of this little chanter is evident only in the hands of he who invented it.[58]

Even though Borjon appears to be writing about the elder Hotteterre rather than one of the 'sons', Jacques Hotteterre le Romain states, in his *Methode pour la musette*, that the little chanter was invented by Martin, his father.[59] Since Borjon's knowledge of the Hotteterres is inexact in other matters, it is Jacques's statement that we probably ought to accept. However this may be, the invention of the little chanter did significantly extend the instrument's capabilities, since previously its range, according to Borjon's own diagram (see Plate I), extended chromatically for only a ninth, from f' to g'', and beyond that diatonically only to the tenth, a''. The little chanter added the $g\sharp''/a\flat''$ that was missing from the large chanter, an additional a'', and $b\flat'''$, b''', c''', and d''', through the addition of six keys, three on each side of the chanter. Those on the front were to be operated by the little finger of the left hand, while those on the back were to be operated by the thumb of the right hand. (Jacques's later method indicated that $e\flat'''$, e''', and f''' could also be produced by opening more than one key at a time, though these notes were little used.) Of all the improvements of woodwind instruments attributed to the Hotteterres, this is the only one of which we can be entirely certain.

Since the musette was very fashionable during the time Martin was making his improvements, we can imagine that he must have been sought out as a teacher by some of the burgeoning numbers of aristocratic amateur players of the instrument. He also composed, but if he wrote pieces suitable for the musette with two chanters, they have disappeared. A simple 'Marche du Regiment de Surlaube' by Martin was printed in his son's musette method, but its diatonic melody encompasses only the range of a sixth, c'' to a'', and does not require the use of the little chanter. In addition, a four-part 'Air des hautbois. fait par M^r. Martin hotteterre' survives in André Philidor's manuscript, 'Partition de Plusieurs Marches et batteries de Tambour tants françoises qu'Etrangères, avec les Airs de fifre et de hautbois à 3 et 4 parties et Pl^{rs}. Marches de timballes et de trompettes à cheval avec les airs de Carousel en 1686, Et les appels et fanfares de trompe pour la Chasse' (1705; Versailles, Ms. Mus. 1163; exact copy, Paris Conservatoire, Rés. F. 671). This air may well have served an organization such as the Grands Hautbois.[60]

The name of Martin's wife, Marie Crespy, is known from a procuration dated 24 April 1696 authorizing her to come to terms, give receipts, make sales and purchases, and do anything else necessary concerning any business she and her husband might have in the region of Normandy. By virtue of this procuration, on 24 September 1696 Madame Hotteterre sold the house in Evreux that Martin's father had bought in 1664, where the sign L'ANCRE NOIR had hung.[61] In 1707 Martin's house on the rue de Harlay du Palais in Paris was marked with the sign of the musette. In 1710 Martin was still listed as a member of the Grands Hautbois; by 1714, when the next records are extant, he had been replaced by his son Jean (V).[62] According to Thoinan, who does not cite the source of his information, Martin died in 1712.[63]

Jacques

Of the next generation of Hotteterres, only Jacques (-Martin) ('Le Romain') (1674-1763) was to achieve fame as an instrument maker. The son of Martin Hotteterre and Marie Crespy, Jacques

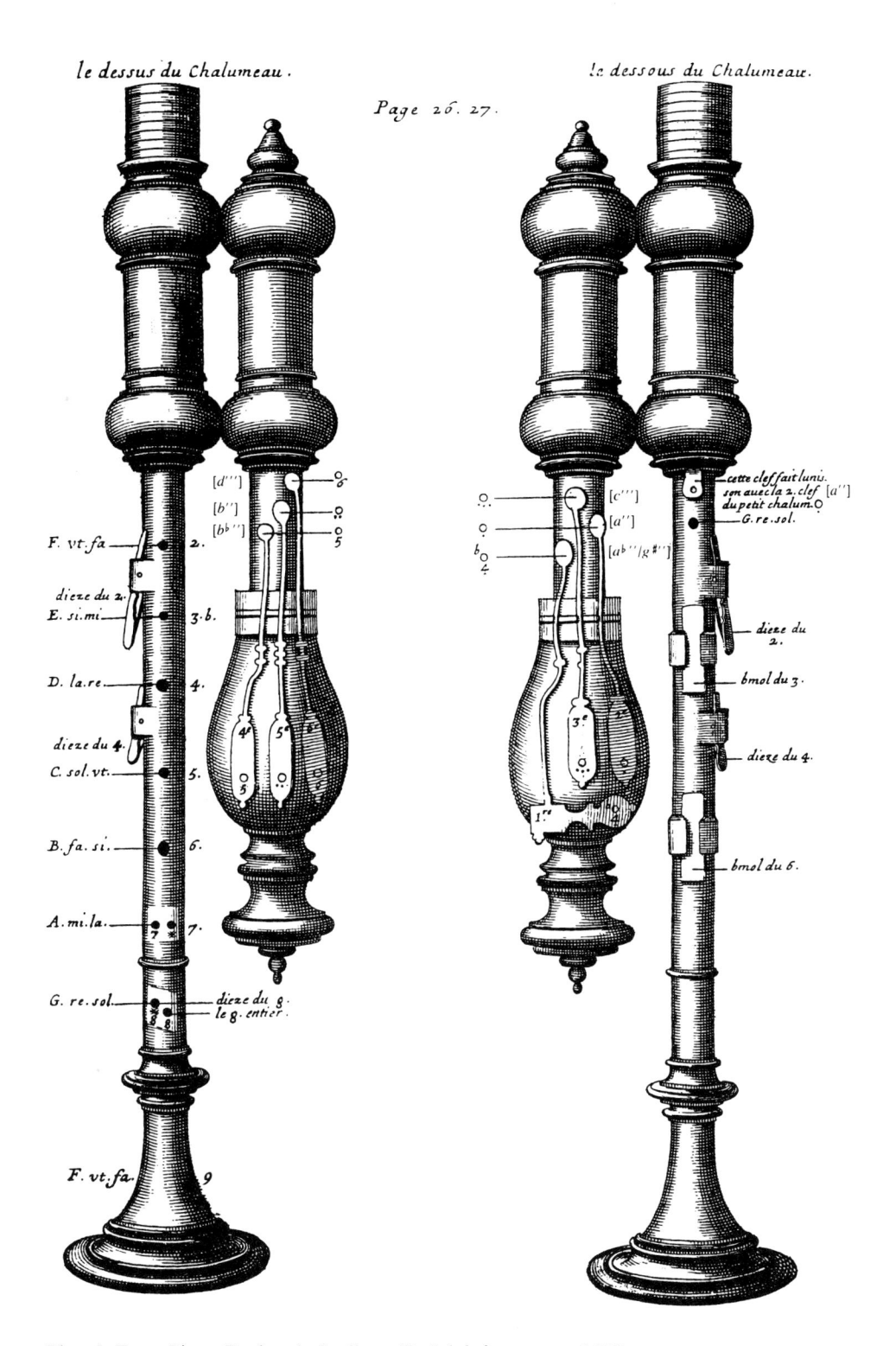

Plate I. From Pierre Borjon de Scellery, *Traité de la musette* (1672)

was born in Paris on 29 September 1674, according to the État Civil Reconstitué of the Archives of the Seine.[64] As early as 1689 he was listed as 'basse de hautbois et basse de violon' in the Grands Hautbois, but only on 21 January 1692, after the death of Jean Ludet, does he seem to have officially succeeded to that post.[65] Although Thoinan asserts that the post went to Jacques-Jean Hotteterre (who is otherwise unknown) at this time, the only contemporary mention of a Jacques-Jean seems to be in *L'État de la France*. In *L'État* of 1699, 'Jâque-Jean Hauteterre' was listed as a member of the Grands Hautbois; in 1705, according to Thoinan, he was still listed, while in the next volume, that of 1708, he was replaced by Jacques Hotteterre le Romain.[66] My guess is that no Jacques-Jean Hotteterre ever existed, and that the same Jacques — Jacques-Martin (whose middle name appears in certain legal documents but never in court records) — belonged to the Grands Hautbois all along. The change of name in *L'État de la France* probably occurred because Jacques had begun to call himself M. Hotteterre Le Romain by this time: the appellation first appears on the title-page of his flute treatise of 1707. While the reason for his choice of the appellation 'Le Romain' is unknown — the suggestion of a possible trip to Italy remaining undocumented, he may well have adopted it upon going into print in order to distinguish himself more clearly from the other members of his family. In any case, support for Jacques's presence in one of the royal musical establishments well before 1708 comes in a couple of documents dated 27 August and 10 September 1694 concerning the appointment of a tutor for Marie-Madeleine, the younger daughter of Nicolas (II) Hotteterre; Jacques, who was present at the appointment, was described as an 'ordinaire de la musique du roi'.[67]

As a flutist, Jacques was already known by the time his *Principes de la flûte traversière* appeared in 1707, for according to an announcement of the treatise which appeared in the *Mémoires de Trévoux* of 1707, 'the name of the author corresponds to the excellence of the book. This capable flutist is not ignorant of any of the secrets of his art'.[68] By 1708 Jacques was 'flûte de la Chambre du Roy', according to the title-page of his *Pièces pour la flûte traversière;* these pieces were dedicated to Louis XIV who had 'deigned to grant' Jacques favorable attention when he had 'had the honor' of playing them in Louis's presence.[69] It was not before 26 August 1717, however, that Jacques received the reversion of the position of 'Joüeur de Fluste de la musique de la chambre' from René Pignon Descoteaux, on the condition that he pay, after the decease of Descoteaux, 6,000 *livres* to his heirs or representative.[70] Although Jacques was listed on the title-pages of all his publications between 1708 and 1717 as 'flûte de la chambre du roi', he had evidently not played for Louis XV (who had succeeded to the throne in 1715) at the time of this reversion, for the document of reversion states that the king had willingly consented to the flutist's appointment, being 'informed of the capacity of the said Hotteterre'.

From the dedications of several of his works, it appears that Jacques was highly sought after as a teacher of the amateurs of the fashionable world; two of his highly placed students were the duke of Orléans and M. du Fargis, the chamberlain of the duke. Further information about Jacques's teaching activities as well as his instrument-making and playing abilities appears in the diary of a German visitor to Paris, J. F. A. von Uffenbach, who described his encounter with Jacques on 25 October 1715 in these terms:

… From here I went to Mr. Hauteterre's, flute du roy, who received me in his quarters on the rue dauphine very politely though somewhat pompously and superciliously. He led me into a tidy room and showed me there many beautiful transverse flutes that he himself makes and from which he wishes to gain special profit. After that he brought forth his musical works, five of

which he has published with considerable applause, and of which I bought one on the instruction of the transverse flute for two livres. After that he showed me another curious instrument improved by him, a musette or sort of bagpipe, which can be tuned in all keys and is very pleasing as well as very fashionable here now. It was ... very costly, covered with velvet and trimmed with wide golden borders and fringes, and also provided with a great many pipes ... and with many silver keys, that make semitones. With another musician who accompanied on the harpsichord, he played a sonata incomparably well and in a completely pleasing manner, with such carefully studied agrements, that I could not hear and admire him enough. I immediately took a fancy to have such a bagpipe, but this disappeared soon when he told me the exact price, namely 10 pistolen. At the same time, however, he also informed me, that he made others without decoration for 5 pistolen. He gives his lessons mostly at home, and charges one pistole an hour, which he spoke of as a trifle. I declined such distinguished instruction and at the same time thanked him for the courtesy he showed me.[71]

Later Uffenbach revisted Jacques in order to purchase some music, and at his request Jacques again played the musette and told Uffenbach which Germans had studied the instrument with him. Thus, Jacques's reputation as a teacher seems to have been international in scope.

Undoubtedly Jacques's reputation as a teacher had been greatly aided by the publication of the instruction book that Uffenbach bought from him, his *Principes de la flûte traversière, ou flûte d'Allemagne, de la flûte à bec, ou flûte douce, et du haut-bois, diviséz par traitéz*. The first treatise on flute playing to appear in any country, it also included instructions for playing the recorder and oboe, and it was a tremendous success both in France, where it was reprinted numerous times, and in other countries, where it appeared in Dutch and English translations.[72] Jacques's pedagogical concerns were to lead him to publish two further treatises — one, *L'Art de préluder sur la flûte traversière, sur la flûte-à-bec, sur le haubois, et autres instrumens de dessus* (1719), which contains preludes and *traits* (practice studies) that stand as rare examples of this art in the literature of the eighteenth-century French flute school, and the other, his *Methode pour la musette* (1737), which is the best method for that instrument written during the eighteenth century.

In addition to his other activities, Jacques composed, primarily for the transverse flute. His pieces, especially his two books of suites for transverse flute and basso continuo (1708, 2/1715; and 1715), a book of trio sonatas (1712), and three duet suites for unaccompanied flutes or other instruments (1712, 1717, and 1722), qualify as some of the most important early compositions for the flute.[73]

Through these years Jacques continued to be active as an instrumentalist at court, sometimes taking part in the Menus Plaisirs (1720, 1721), and sometimes going to Fontainebleau to play in concerts 'faits ches la Reyne'.[74] His reputation as a performer must have been considerable, for in 1743 Titon du Tillet included him in his 'Orchestre du Parnasse' made up of the most famous musicians of France.[75] In the mid-forties, Jacques made plans to pass on his royal charges to two of his sons, and on 1 June 1746 he gave the reversion of his place in the Grands Hautbois to his son Antoine-Jacques, and on 20 December 1747, the reversion of his position as 'flûte de la musique de la chambre' to his son Jean-Baptiste. On 2 May 1747, however, Antoine-Jacques died at the age of thirteen,[76] and on 7 July 1748 Jean-Baptiste gained the reversion of the Grands Hautbois post too.[77] Nevertheless, Jacques's name continued to figure in royal accounts as late as 1761, according to Thoinan. He died on 16 July 1763; his death date is recorded in the Archives Nationales.[78]

The Instruments

Even though some members of the Hotteterre family in the generation after Jacques's continued to work as instrument makers, none, except for the above-mentioned musette-making Chédevilles, were active in Paris. For obvious reasons, those working in small towns did not garner the fame that their Parisian predecessors had. But it may still be that one or more of the surviving Hotteterre instruments were made by one of the later family members. In considering the extant instruments, we should keep in mind that the Hotteterre craftsmen were active between approximately 1640, around which date Jean (I) may have begun his work in Paris, and the latter part of the eighteenth century, when Philippe (II) (1714-1773) and Louis (VI) (1717-1801) were presumably still working. Nevertheless, the most intensive period of Hotteterre instrument making would probably have finished no later than around 1730, with the deaths of Nicolas (III) and Jean (III). Although Jacques lived until 1763, he may have ceased making instruments well before this, since the three surviving Hotteterre transverse flutes, of all the instruments the ones most likely to have come from his workshop, belong to the earliest types of one-keyed flutes known and would probably not have been made much past 1720, if that late.[79]

Currently, eighteen instruments made by members of the Hotteterre family are known. These include three transverse flutes, two oboes, and thirteen recorders, among which there are five altos, five tenors, and three basses. Although the instruments are stamped with a variety of marks, none of which can be matched decisively with a particular maker, the nature of some of the marks, especially when considered in connection with other information, allows some reasonable speculations to be made about which makers used each mark.

Four instruments seem to be marked with a six-pointed star over the name HOTTÉTERRE, including an alto recorder in the Rosenbaum collection, a three-keyed oboe in the Brussels Musée Instrumental (No. 2320), a tenor recorder which formerly belonged to M. Petit of Blois, and a bass recorder in the possession of Laurent Kaltenbach in Paris.[80] (On the Brussels instrument, however, the marks are very worn, and the presence of the N is not entirely certain.) Because of the initial N, the brand might have belonged to any of the three Nicolas Hotteterres, or might have been used by all three, since they were closely related and the two sons worked with their father for at least some period of time. Since Nicolas (III), however, had by far the longest working period of the three, seems to have run by far the largest operation (if the tools and materials inventoried after his wife's death in 1708 and his own in 1727 fairly represent its size and scope), and was among the leading makers in Paris according to Du Pradel, he seems to be the most likely of the three to have adopted an individual mark. In addition, the relatively late design of the oboe marked HOTTÉTERRE[81] may point to Nicolas (III), since Nicolas (I) and Nicolas (II) had died in the early 1690s. I would therefore tentatively suggest that the instruments bearing the six-pointed star over HOTTÉTERRE were made by Nicolas (III).[82] Another instrument — a maple bass recorder with ivory rings at the Paris Conservatoire which formerly belonged to Madame de Chambure (E. 979.2.10) — is marked with a six-pointed star over the name HOTTETERRE, and over the first E in the name are the remnants of an initial that is now too effaced to read.[83] Perhaps this instrument too belongs to the output of the Nicolas Hotteterre whose mark was a six-pointed star over the name HOTTÉTERRE.

Two other instruments — an alto recorder in the Deutsches Museum, Munich (No. 63053), and another in the Dayton C. Miller Collection, Library of Congress, Washington D.C. (No. 326) — are marked with a fleur-de-lis over the name HOTTÉTERRE.[84] The three Louis Hotteterres known as instrument makers or 'tourneurs' to whom this mark might have belonged were Louis (IV), Louis (V), and Louis (VI). Since Louis (V) was the best known of these three and the only one who lived in Paris, where the custom of marking instruments was stronger than in the country, it seems likely, on the one hand, that he may have adopted this mark. On the other hand, he signed his name 'Louis Hautteterre',[85] and thus it is perhaps just as likely that the mark on an alto recorder in the possession of Hansheiner Ritz — HAVTETERRE on the head joint and LH on the foot joint — was his.[86] Since Louis (IV) signed his name 'Louis Hauterre', Mauger has suggested that a tenor recorder in the Leningrad collection (No. 405), the only surviving instrument marked with the name HAUTERRE (with a little fleur-de-lis below), belongs to his output.[87] The mark HOTTĒTERRE without a fleur-de-lis which appears on a two-keyed oboe in the possession of the Toho School of Music, Tokyo, seems, however, to have belonged to Louis (VI) (1717-1801) since the instrument is too late in design to have come from the workshop of any of the early Louises.[88] There are thus more surviving marks that seem to point to different Louises than there were Louis Hotteterres who are known to have been instrument makers. Was one of the other Louises active in this profession as well, or did one of them change his mark?

The mark of an anchor below the name HOTTETERRE which appears on eight surviving instruments is just as problematical. I have already mentioned Thoinan's theory that the sign of the anchor was first adopted by Jean (I), and that it was then passed down to Jean's son Martin and grandson Jacques. Although this matter remains speculative, the number of instruments bearing the sign of an anchor may give some credibility to the suggestion that the mark was shared by several makers in the same line of descent. Other evidence may suggest Jacques as the maker of at least some of the instruments bearing this mark. Among the instruments marked with an anchor below the name HOTTETERRE are the only three surviving transverse flutes attributable to the family (Musikinstrumenten-Museum, Berlin, No. 2670; Institute of the Theater, Music, and Cinematography, Leningrad, No. 471; and Landesmuseum Joanneum, Graz, No.1384). With their ivory head caps, ivory ferrules, and ivory foot joints (the latter feature pertaining only to the Berlin and Leningrad flutes), these flutes are among the most elegant instruments of their type known today.[89] Since Jacques was a distinguished flutist, and the report of Uffenbach quoted above specifically mentions the 'many beautiful transverse flutes that he himself [Jacques] makes and from which he wishes to gain special profit', it is tempting to associate the surviving elegant flutes with Jacques, rather than with another well-known and productive maker such as Jean (III). The possibility that they were made by Jean (III) certainly cannot be ruled out, nevertheless. That they were, however, made by the same maker rather than by two or more makers sharing the same mark seems evident because of close similarities in the measurements of the three instruments.[90]

No doubt other Hotteterres besides the one or ones who used the mark of the anchor also fashioned elegant instruments for customers who wished them. Whoever used the anchor, however, may have made more a specialty of this than the others, since to his output also belongs the only surviving Hotteterre instrument made entirely of ivory — an alto recorder in the Musée Instrumental of the Paris Conservatoire which formerly belonged to Madame de Chambure (E. 979.2.8).[91] But the remaining four instruments that are marked Hotteterre above an anchor — a maple tenor recorder with ivory rings and beak in the Paris Conservatoire collection (E. 590, C. 402), a second maple or fruitwood tenor recorder there that formerly belonged to Madame de Chambure (E. 979.2.9), a tenor recorder in the collection of Frans Brüggen, and a maple (?) bass recorder with ivory rings also in Paris (E. 589, C. 413)[92] — offer no very suggestive clues as to their probable maker. To all appearances, we may as well accept Thoinan's intuitive theory about this mark being passed down from Jean (I) to Martin to Jacques (although at the same time we ought not to forget the productivity of Jean [III]). Some of the recorders bearing the anchor may well date back to the time of Jean (I), when recorders of various sizes were in frequent use in the opera orchestra, while the one-keyed flutes, whose use cannot be documented before around 1680 and which did not become widely used before the early years of the eighteenth century,[93] point to the time of Jacques's activity as a maker.

While numerous questions still remain about the paternity of the surviving Hotteterre family instruments and the precise activities of individual makers, slow progress has been made through the years in shedding greater light on both these matters. The concluding table of all Hotteterre instruments known at present may help put the surviving work of the family into clearer perspective.[94]

Extant Hotteterre Instruments

Mark	Materials	Location
Recorders: Alto		
1. 6-pointed star above N HOTTETERRE (on all 3 joints)	Boxwood with imitation tortoise-shell design	Collection of Dorothy and Robert Rosenbaum, Scarsdale, N.Y., No. 3
2. Fleur-de-lis above ·L· HOTTETERRE (head joint by J. C. Denner)	Ebony with ivory rings and beak	Deutsches Museum, Munich, No. 63053
3. Fleur-de-lis above ·L· HOTTETERRE (on all 3 joints)	Boxwood with ivory rings and beak	Dayton C. Miller Collection, Library of Congress, Washington, D.C., No. 326
4. HOTTETERRE with an anchor below (on all 3 joints)	Ivory	Musée Instrumental du Conservatoire National Supérieur de Musique, Paris, No. E. 979.2.8 (formerly Chambure)
5. HAVTETERRE (on head joint only); LH (on foot joint only)	Boxwood	Collection of Hansheiner Ritz, Nordenham, West Germany

Recorders: Tenor

1. 6-pointed star above
   N
   HOTTETERRE

   ?

   Formerly belonged to M. Petit of Blois; present whereabouts unverified

2. HOTTETERRE with an anchor below

   Maple with ivory rings and beak; one brass key

   Musée Instrumental, Paris, No. E. 590, C. 402

3. HOTTETERRE with an anchor below (on head joint only)

   Black ebony with ivory rings and beak; one silver key

   Collection of Frans Brüggen, Amsterdam

4. HAUTERRE over a fleur-de-lis (on all 3 joints); HOTTETERRE over a fleur-de-lis (also on foot joint)

   Boxwood?; one brass key

   Institute of the Theatre, Music, and Cinematography, Leningrad, No. 405

5. HOTTETERRE with an anchor below (visible only on the foot joint)

   Maple or fruitwood with one ivory ring; one brass key

   Musée Instrumental, Paris, No. E. 979.2.9 (formerly Chambure)

Recorders: Bass

1. HOTTETERRE with an anchor below (on all 3 joints)

   Maple? with ivory rings; one brass key; brass crook

   Musée Instrumental, Paris, No. E. 589, C. 413

2. 6-pointed star above
   (?)
   HOTTETERRE
   (mark over Hotteterre too effaced to read)

   Maple or fruitwood with ivory rings; one brass key; brass crook

   Musée Instrumental, Paris, No. E. 979, 2.10 (formerly Chambure)

3. 6-pointed star above
   N
   HOTTETERRE
   (on all 3 joints)

   Fruitwood with ivory rings; one brass key; brass crook

   Collection of Laurent Kaltenbach, Paris

Oboes

1. 6-pointed star above
   N (?)
   HOTTETERRE
   (on head and middle joints; bell by Debey)

   Boxwood with ivory rings; three brass keys

   Musée Instrumental du Conservatoire Royal de Musique, Brussels, No. 2320

2. L.
   HOTTETERRE
   (on uppermost joint)

   Boxwood with ivory rings; two silver keys

   Toho School of Music, Tokyo

Transverse Flutes

1. HOTTETERRE with an anchor below (on head and middle joints)	Boxwood with ivory head cap, foot joint, and ring; one silver key	Musikinstrumenten-Museum des Staatlichen Institut für Musikforschung, Berlin, No. 2670
2. HOTTETERRE with an anchor below	Boxwood with ivory head cap, foot joint, and ring; one siver key	Institute of the Theater, Music, and Cinematography, Leningrad, No. 471
3. HOTTETERRE with an anchor below (on head and middle joints)	Ebony with ivory head cap and rings; one silver key	Landesmuseum Joanneum, Graz, No. 1384

Notes

1 See, for example, Anthony Baines, *Woodwind Instruments and their History*, 3rd ed. (London: Faber and Faber, 1967), pp. 273-78, 286, and 290-91; and Philip Bate, *The Flute: A Study of its History, Development and Construction* (London: Ernest Benn, 1969), pp. 77-80.

2 'Mémoire de M. de La Barre: Sur les musettes et hautbois &c.', in *Écrits de musiciens*, ed. J.-G. Prod'homme (Paris: Mercure de France, 1912), p. 244; see also Marcelle Benoit, *Musiques de cour: Chapelle, chambre, écurie, 1661-1733* (Paris: A. & J. Picard, 1971), p. 455; and Jane M. Bowers, '*Flaüste traverseinne* and *Flûte d'Allemagne* — The Flute in France from the Late Middle Ages up through 1702', *'Recherches' sur la Musique française classique* 19 (1979): 33.

3 *Traité de la musette, avec une nouvelle méthode, pour apprendre de soy-mesme à jouer de cet instrument facilement, & en peu de temps* (Lyon: Jean Girin & Barthelemy Riviere, 1672), p. 38.

4 Abraham Du Pradel [Nicolas de Blegny], *Le Livre commode des adresses de Paris pour 1692*, ed. Edouard Fournier, 2 vols. (Paris: Paul Daffis, 1878), 1:212 and 2:72.

5 See Nicolas Mauger, *Les Hotteterre: Célèbres joueurs et facteurs de flûtes, hautbois, bassons et musettes des XVIIe et XVIIIe siècles. Nouvelles recherches* (Paris: Fischbacher, 1912), pp. 18-19 and 30-32.

6 See Mauger, pp. 26-27.

7 See Ernest Thoinan [Antoine Ernest Roquet], *Les Hotteterre et les Chédeville, célèbres joueurs et facteurs de flûtes, hautbois, bassons et musettes des XVIIe et XVIIIe siècles* (Paris: Sagot, 1894), pp. 44-45; and Mauger, p. 27.

8 See Thoinan, p. 45; and Mauger, p. 27.

9 See Thoinan, p. 45; and Mauger, p. 28.

10 Mauger, p. 15.

11 Yolande de Brossard, *Musiciens de Paris, 1535-1792: Actes d'état civil d'après le Fichier La Borde de la Bibliothèque Nationale* (Paris: A. & J. Picard, 1965), p. 151.

12 Madeleine Jurgens, *Documents du Minutier central concernant l'histoire de la musique, 1600-1650*, vol. 2 (Paris: La Documentation Française, 1974), p. 754.

13 Brossard, p. 50.

14 Michel de Marolles, 'De l'excellence de la ville de Paris', *Mémoires*, 2nd ed. (Amsterdam: Goujet, 1755); reprinted in *Paris ou description de cette ville*, ed. Valentin Dufour (Paris: A. Quantin, 1879), p. 319.

15 Thoinan, pp. 16 and 19; and Benoit, *Musiques de cour*, pp. 17-18.

16 Thoinan, pp. 11 and 15-16.

17 Jacques Hotteterre, *Methode pour la musette*, op. 10 (Paris: J.-B. Ballard, 1737), pp. 64-65.

18 Thoinan, pp. 18-19. See Mauger, p. 20, for the land at La Couture Jean (I) bought in 1657.

19 Mauger, p. 16.

20 Thoinan, p. 18.

21 Mauger, pp. 16-17.

22 An entry in the death register of the city of Versailles states that Nicolas (II) was around fifty-seven years old at the time of his death on 10 May 1694; see Mauger, p. 33.

23 *Œuvres complètes de J.-B. Lully: Les Ballets, tome I*, ed. Henry Prunières (Paris: Editions de la Revue Musicale, 1931), p. 42.

24 Thoinan, p. 21.

25 Benoit, *Musiques de cour*, p. 15.

26 Mauger, p. 18.

27 Mauger, p. 31. Whether or not Jean (IV) worked alongside his father and brothers as an instrument maker is not known, but it seems only reasonable to assume that he would have done so. Although he is not mentioned in the declaration made by his mother Anne Mauger in 1693, that was undoubtedly because he was no longer living. On his playing in the Grands Hautbois, see Thoinan, p. 32; Mauger, pp. 35-37 (both Thoinan and Mauger refer to him as Jean III); and Benoit, *Musiques de cour*, pp. 24, 56, 74, 85, and 87.

28 The original document is quoted in Mauger, pp. 31-32; I wish to thank John Eric Swenson for helping me translate this document as well as others consulted for this study.
Several documents shedding light on the equalization of the inheritances of Louis (V) and Nicolas (III) are listed among the papers inventoried after the death of Nicolas (III); see Marcelle Benoit and Norbert Dufourcq, 'Documents du Minutier Central: Musiciens français du XVIIIe siècle', *'Recherches' sur la Musique française classique* 10 (1970): 211 and 213-14.

29 Mauger, pp. 30-31.

30 Benoit, *Musiques de cour*, pp. 96, 121, and 139-40; and Mauger, p. 33. Two documents quoted by Benoit indicate that Nicolas (II)'s post in the Grands Hautbois was taken over by Jean Hannès Desjardins only after Nicolas's death, although another dated 1689 shows his name crossed out and replaced by that of Desjardins.

31 Norbert Dufourcq and Marcelle Benoit, 'Les Musiciens de Versailles à travers les minutes notariales de Lamy versées aux Archives Départementales de Seine-et-Oise', *'Recherches' sur la Musique française classique* 3 (1963): 193.

32 Thoinan, pp. 21-22.

33 Ibid., pp. 28-29.

34 Marcelle Benoit, *Versailles et les musiciens du roi, 1661-1733: Étude institutionnelle et sociale* (Paris: A. et J. Picard, 1971), p. 109; and Benoit, *Musiques de cour*, pp. 15, 256, 258, and 278.

35 Du Pradel, 2:72.

36 Benoit and Dufourcq, 'Documents', *'Recherches'* 10: 210-12. Various contracts of the sale of property to Louis (V) passed into the possession of Nicolas (III) after Louis's death and are listed in the inventory made after Nicolas's death. See also Mauger, p. 27.

37 Mauger, p. 34; and Benoit and Dufourcq, 'Documents', *'Recherches'* 10:211.

38 The date of 10 February 1653 given for Nicolas (III)'s baptism in Benoit and Dufourcq, 'Documents', *'Recherches'* 10:209, is a misprint (personal communication from Marcelle Benoit).

39 Among the papers inventoried after Nicolas (III)'s death, according to Benoit and Dufourcq, 'Documents', *'Recherches'* 10:210, were a *brevet de hautbois de la Grande Ecurie* accorded by the king to Nicolas on 9 October 1686 and the *prestation de serment* (oath-taking) dated 15 October 1686. But 1686 seems to be a misprint for 1666; in Benoit, *Musiques de cour*, Nicolas (III)'s presence in the Grands Hautbois is documented from 1667 on. See the same source, p. 373, for Nicolas's death date.

40 Thoinan, pp. 30-31. See also Jérôme de La Gorce, 'L'Académie Royal de Musique en 1704, d'après des documents inédits conservés dans les archives notariales', *Revue de musicologie* 15 (1979): 178, for Nicolas (III)'s presence (he is listed as 'C. hauterre') in the opera orchestra at a somewhat earlier period.

41 Mauger, p. 34; and Marcelle Benoit and Norbert Dufourcq, 'Documents du Minutier Central: Musiciens français du XVIIIe siècle', *'Recherches' sur la Musique française classique* 9 (1969): 217 and 220. Catherine was 'about 14 years old' when her mother died in 1708.

42 Many contracts of sale and leases are listed in the inventory made after Nicolas (III)'s decease; see Benoit and Dufourcq, 'Documents', *'Recherches'* 10:210-13. The fief at Serez is described in Mauger, p. 35.

43 For the 1708 inventory, see Benoit and Dufourcq, 'Documents', *'Recherches'* 9:217-20.

44 Du Pradel, 1:212.

45 For the entire inventory, see Benoit and Dufourcq, 'Documents', *'Recherches'* 10:203-14. The instruments are listed on pp. 204 and 207.

46 For the will, see ibid., pp. 202-3. Both dates appear in the sources.

47 Ibid., pp. 203 and 214.

48 On the Chédevilles, see especially Thoinan, pp. 49-54; and Jane M. Bowers, 'Chédeville', *The New Grove Dictionary of Music and Musicians*, ed. Stanley Sadie (London: Macmillan, 1980), 4:189-90. The only existing musette marked CHEDEVILLE known today is in the Brussels Musée Instrumental (No. 1125).

49 When Jean (III) was discovered missing in 1732, the relatives who applied to the civil authorities for help said that he was eighty-four years old; see below.

50 Thoinan, pp. 32-34.

51 Benoit, *Musiques de cour*, pp. 85 and 87.

52 Ibid., pp. 337, 350, and 352.

53 Du Pradel, 1:212; and Joseph Sauveur, *Principes d'acoustique et de musique, ou système général des intervalles des sons: inseré dans les Mémoires de 1701 de l'Académie royale des sciences* (?Paris, n.d.), p. 37.

54 Benoit and Dufourcq, 'Documents', *'Recherches'* 10:202.

55 Thoinan, pp. 35-36.

56 Ibid., p. 22.

57 After 1699 the records of the Hautbois et Musettes usually read 'Martin Hotteterre et Jean Hotteterre son fils en survivance'; see Benoit, *Musiques de cour*, pp. 174, 188, and 199. On the other points, see ibid., pp. 13, 15, 17-18, 164, 166, and passim.

58 *Traité de la musette*, pp. 25 and 27; see also Thoinan, pp. 24-26.

59 P. 64.

60 Both the march and the air are printed in Thoinan, pp. 26-27.

61 Mauger, p. 22.

62 Benoit, *Musiques de cour*, pp. 219 and 263.

63 Thoinan, p. 28.

64 There are two entries in the État Civil Reconstitué for Jacques's birthdate — 29 September 1673 and 29 September 1674; John Hajdu, who has studied both entries closely, believes that the latter date is the correct one (personal communication to the author).

65 Benoit, *Musiques de cour*, pp. 121 and 131.

66 *L'État de la France* (Paris: Charles Osmont, 1699), p. 561; and Thoinan, p. 62.

67 Norbert Dufourcq and Marcelle Benoit, 'Les Musiciens de Versailles à travers les minutes du Bailliage de Versailles conservées aux Archives Départementales de Seine-et-Oise', *'Recherches' sur la Musique française classique* 6 (1966): 201.

68 *Mémoires pour l'histoire des sciences et des beaux arts* (Trévoux: Etienne Ganeau), Aug. 1707, pp. 1487-88.

69 *Pièces pour la flûte traversière, et autres instruments, avec la basse continue... Livre premier. Œuvre second* (Paris: Christophe Ballard, 1708), dedication.

70 Benoit, *Musiques de cour*, p. 283. A brevet of 27 September 1718, however, makes it clear that Descoteaux could also dispose of the 6,000 *livres* in his own lifetime if he so chose; see ibid., p. 294.

71 Eberhard Preussner, *Die musikalischen Reisen des Herrn von Uffenbach* (Kassel: Bärenreiter, 1949), pp. 128-29.

72 For listings of the various editions, see especially Jane Bowers, 'A Catalogue of French Works for the Transverse Flute, 1692-1761', *'Recherches' sur la Musique française classique* 18 (1978): 124-25; and Thomas E. Warner, *An Annotated Bibliography of Woodwind Instruction Books, 1600-1830,* Detroit Studies in Music Bibliography 11 (Detroit: Information Coordinators, Inc., 1967), pp. 9 and 13.

73 For additional information on Jacques's works, see Jane M. Bowers, 'Hotteterre', *The New Grove Dictionary* 8: 736; and idem, 'Catalogue', pp. 100, 108, and 115.

74 Benoit, *Musiques de cour,* pp. 314, 322, and 365.

75 Evrard Titon de Tillet, *Supplément de Parnasse françois jusqu'en cette année 1743* (Paris: Coignard, n.d.), p. 675.

76 Paris, Archives Nationales, O^1 871, no. 151, extract from the registers of St. Sulpice. According to O^1 871, no. 67, Antoine-Jacques was born on 2 July 1733.

77 Various documents disagree on the precise dates on which the reversions were granted; those given here are taken from Robert Machard, 'Les Musiciens de France au temps de Jean-Philippe Rameau, d'après les actes du Secrétariat de la Maison du Roi', *'Recherches' sur la Musique française classique* 11 (1971): 85, 93, and 94, which are based on Paris, Archives Nationales, O^1 90, O^1 91, and O^1 92. Those given by O^1 872, nos. 39 and 40, agree with those of O^1 90 and O^1 92 while slightly varying dates are found in O^1 871, nos. 66, 68, 150, and 153.

78 O^1 872, no. 49, p. 28.

79 For the different stages in the development of the one-keyed flute, see Jane M. Bowers, 'New Light on the Development of the Transverse Flute between about 1650 and about 1770', *Journal of the American Musical Instrument Society* 3 (1977): 5-56.

80 For the alto recorder, see Graham Wells, 'London Salesrooms Report', *Early Music* 2 (1974): 176-77; Phillip T. Young, *The Look of Music: Rare Musical Instruments, 1500-1900* (Vancouver: Vancouver Museums & Planetarium Association, 1980), p. 71 (no. 53); and the forthcoming *Pythagoras at the Forge: An Annotated Catalogue of the Rosenbaum Collection of Western European Musical Instruments*, ed. Robert M. Rosenbaum. Neither Wells nor Young mentions the N in the mark; it was discovered by Phillip Young only after the instrument arrived in Vancouver for *The Look of Music* exhibition. I am deeply indebted to Mr. Young for sharing with me his knowledge about this mark, as well as the one on the Brussels oboe; indeed, he generously provided me with information about all the extant Hotteterre instruments. I am also indebted to René de Maeyer, Director of the Musée Instrumental in Brussels, for sharing with me information about the oboe's mark.

For the oboe, see Victor-Charles Mahillon, *Catalogue descriptif et analytique du Musée instrumental (historique et technique) du Conservatoire Royal de Musique de Bruxelles*, vol. 4 (Ghent: Ad. Hoste, 1912), pp. 194-95; Anthony Baines, *European and American Musical Instruments* (New York: The Viking Press, 1966), pp. 104-5 (no. 550); and Young, *The Look of Music*, p. 74 (no. 60), where a good photograph of it appears. The original foot joint of the instrument has been replaced by one marked Debey.

For the tenor recorder, see Thoinan, p. 21. For all of the above instruments, see also Phillip T. Young, *Twenty-Five Hundred Historical Woodwind Instruments: An Inventory of the Major Collections* (New York: Pendragon Press, 1982), p. 67, where, however, some of the stars are erroneously said to be five-pointed.

For information about the bass recorder, I am very much indebted to Phillip Young who generously shared with me his observations made from personal inspection of the instrument, and to its owner, Laurent Kaltenbach, who sent me a photograph of the recorder and answered many of my questions about it.

81 See Young, *The Look of Music*, p. 74. The date suggested by Young (circa 1720?), however, is largely a guess (personal communication to the author).

82 A fourth Nicolas Hotteterre (1720-c1759) who was the son of Philippe (I) and the grandson of Louis (IV) must also be mentioned. It is certainly possible that he too worked as an instrument maker, since in addition to his father and grandfather, two of his brothers, Philippe (II) and Louis (VI), were known as such. But it seems inconceivable that an unknown maker fashioned the four extant instruments marked HOTT$\overset{N}{E}$TERRE while distinguished and active makers left none behind (at least with marks that point to them).

83 The instrument and mark are depicted in G. Thibault (Mme de Chambure), Jean Jenkins, and Josiane Bran-Ricci, *Eighteenth Century Musical Instruments: France and Britain* (London: Victoria & Albert Museum, 1973), p. 126 (nos. 77 and 77a), and they are described in *Musiques anciennes: Instruments et partitions (XVIe-XVIIe siècles)*, comp. Josiane Bran-Ricci et al (Paris: Bibliothèque Nationale, 1980), pp. 66-67 (no. 32), without, however, the effaced initial being mentioned. Phillip Young has also noted a remarkable similarity between the middle and foot joints of this instrument and those of the bass recorder belonging to Laurent Kaltenbach which is marked HOTT$\overset{N}{E}$TERRE (personal communication to author).

84 See Heinrich Seifers, *Die Blasinstrumente im Deutschen Museum: Beschreibender Katalog*, Deutsches Museum, Abhandlungen und Berichte, 44. Jahrgang, Heft 1 (Munich: R. Oldenbourg Verlag, 1976), p. 23 (where, however, the fleur-de-lis on the Munich instrument is not mentioned); *Musical Instruments in the Dayton C. Miller Flute Collection at the Library of Congress: A Catalog, Volume I: Recorders, Fifes, and Simple System Transverse Flutes of One Key*, comp. Michael Seyfrit (Washington: Library of Congress, 1982), p. 20 (no. 18) and plate IV; and Young, *The Look of Music*, p. 71 (no. 54). Photographs of the mark on the Dayton C. Miller recorder appear in both the Dayton C. Miller *Catalog* and Young.

85 Mauger, p. 34.

86 I am indebted to Mr. Ritz for generously supplying me with a photograph of and information about his recorder. The middle joint appears not to be signed, and it was probably also shortened at one time.

87 In addition to the mark HAUTERRE which appears on all three joints, the instrument bears the mark HOTTETERRE over a fleur-de-lis right above the other mark on the foot joint of the

instrument. This seems to be the recorder which Thoinan owned and described in his book on p. 18. The marks on the foot joint are depicted in Young, *The Look of Music*, p. 72 (no. 55).

88 This oboe seems to be the same as the one described by Thoinan, p. 29, which was formerly in the possession of Count Adhémar. More recently it belonged to Frans Brüggen and is attributed to his collection in Young, *2500 Historical Woodwind Instruments*, p. 67, but it was sold by Brüggen to the Toho School of Music (personal communication to the author). It is depicted in Young, plate VIII.

89 On the flutes, see Bowers, 'New Light', pp. 12-16 and 22-23; Curt Sachs, *Sammlung alter Musikinstrumente bei der Staatliche Hochschule für Musik zu Berlin: Beschreibender Katalog* (Berlin: Julius Bard, 1922), col. 255 and plate 25 (no. 2670); Baines, *European and American Musical Instruments*, p. 86 (no. 466); and Young, *The Look of Music*, pp. 24 (no. 58) and 74 (no. 59). The 'Hotteterre' flute at La Couture-Boussey mentioned by Bowers, p. 13, following Thibault, Jenkins, and Bran-Ricci, p. 135 (no. 87), is not an original instrument, according to information given the author by Mme Bran-Ricci; it is part of a collection of copies made at La Couture-Boussey in the nineteenth century in order to form a sort of retrospective museum of the manufacture of wind instruments.

90 Personal communication from Friedrich von Huene.

91 The instrument is depicted in Thibault, Jenkins, and Bran-Ricci, pp. 120-21 (no. 73), and is described in *Musiques anciennes:* pp. 65-66 (no. 30).

92 For the three recorders in Paris, see Young, *The Look of Music*, p. 73 (nos. 56 and 57); Thibault, Jenkins, and Bran-Ricci, p. 124 (no. 75); Bob Marvin, 'Recorders and English Flutes in European Collections', *Galpin Society Journal* 25 (1972): 39-40; *Musiques anciennes*, p. 66 (no. 31); and Gustave Chouquet, *Le Musée du Conservatoire National de Musique: Catalogue descriptif et raisonée*, nouvelle édition (Paris: Firmin-Didot et Cie, 1884), pp. 104-5 and 107. For the recorder in Frans Brüggen's collection, see Young, *2500 Historical Woodwind Instruments*, p. 66 and plate VIII; and *The Recorder Collection of Frans Brüggen. Drawings by Frederick Morgan* (Tokyo: Zen-On Music Company, Ltd., 1981), pp. 6-7 and Drawing Sheet No. II, where precise measurements, drawings, and a photograph of this instrument may be found.

93 See Bowers, 'New Light', pp. 9-12, and idem, *'Flaüste traverseinne'*, pp. 34-49.

94 A maple alto recorder listed by Marvin (p. 40) as being in the collection of Madame de Chambure does not appear in the catalogue describing the instruments which passed from her collection into that of the Musée Instrumental, Paris, after her death. In a personal communication to the author, Marvin admitted that he erroneously listed the bass recorder in Madame de Chambure's collection, which he did not mention, as an alto. Thus the problem of this phantom sixth Hotteterre alto recorder (see Young, *2500 Historical Woodwind Instruments*, p. 66) has been solved.

The performance of trills in french baroque dance music

Betty Bang Mather

[In the choice of ornaments], good taste is the only law that one can follow.
Saint-Lambert, 1702 (p. 42)[1]

Despite Saint-Lambert's words and the obvious importance of good taste, he and many other Baroque authors gave rules on the choice of ornaments and on the manner of their performance. Moreover, the written-out ornaments in large or small notation often encountered in dance pieces provides additional information on their use.

Trills have a number of possible functions in dance pieces as in other music. Trills can accent dance rhythms even on instruments unable to make dynamic contrasts. They can sustain notes on instruments whose sound otherwise decays. They can imitate the trembling voice of a speaker influenced by an intense passion. And they can aid the flow of a melody as it moves toward a repose, or arrest the flow just before or at a repose.

Trills may emphasize specific notes or they may group two or more notes together. A trill begun on the beat seems to accent the beat. A trill begun in the time of the previous note seems to group the note bearing the trill sign with its previous note. A suffix on a trill seems to group its note with the following one. Brief trills mark and decorate points of repose, or bring out the offbeat stresses that characterize some types of dances. Long trills draw attention to certain notes and thus help sustain interest in the musical line.

This article addresses only those points about trills that relate directly to dance music. Chapters 24 and 25 of Frederick Neumann's *Ornamentation in Baroque and Post-Baroque Music*[2] offer a number of pertinent examples that are recommended for further study. His terminology is used here.

1 Simple trill
An ornament in which the main note alternates with its upper auxiliary.

2 Simple trill with suffix
A simple trill followed by a suffix of one or two notes: the one-note suffix has the pitch of the following note; the two-note suffix adds the pitch of the lower auxiliary and then repeats the pitch of the main note.

3 Compound trill
A trill preceded by a turn, a slide or a mordent, each of which includes the pitch of the lower auxiliary.

4 Trill with onbeat start
A trill that starts at the time notated.

5 Trill with prebeat start
A trill that starts before the time notated.

6 Main-note trill
A trill that starts with the pitch of the main note.

7 Appoggiatura trill
An onbeat trill beginning with the upper note.

8 Trill with main-note anchoring
A trill in which the main note is emphasized in the mind of the performer during the alternations; the main note of the alternations may be slightly increased in length or loudness, or both.

9 Trill with upper-note anchoring
A trill in which the upper-note is emphasized as an appoggiatura during the alternations.

10 Accelerated trill
A trill in which the alternations begin slowly and then gradually increase in speed.

11 Supported trill
A trill whose first note is lengthened before the alternations start.

12 Grace-note trill
A trill with the initial upper note played before the beat and the main note played on the beat.

13 Anticipated trill
A trill whose alternations take place in the time of the preceding note.

14 Straddling trill
A trill whose alternations are divided between the times of the preceding note and the note bearing the sign for a trill.

15 Trill with rest point
A trill whose alternations stop before the end of the note; the rest point (Couperin's *point d'arrêt*) is on the pitch of the main note.

Ornamentation charts of the 17th and 18th centuries almost invariably specify trills in rigid rhythmic patterns. But performing trills in a carefully calculated rhythm and with unvarying loudness (especially on instruments capable of varying loudness) weakens the rhythmic 'swing', the expression of the passion, or both. Indeed trills may express bursts of happiness, anger or grief in dance songs and instrumental pieces.

Lully's Trills
Lully notated few ornaments in his dance music. Those he does show are notated with a trill sign or are written out in large note values. The evidence of his contemporaries and especially of Jean Rousseau's tutors for voice[3] and for viol da gamba[4] reveal that most trills in the dance music of Lully's day begin on the main note or before the beat. Only a few may start with the upper note and on the beat.

Borjon in his musette tutor of 1672[5] indicates only main-note trills. Jean Rousseau in both tutors (vocal, p. 56; viol, p. 84) says that, in all possible situations (*en toutes rencontres*) in gay pieces such as menuets, trills may begin on the main note. He adds that if a trill is begun instead with the upper note, the upper note must be very light (*léger*). He mentions also that main-note trills may be used in other pieces, but that taste must be the guide. The trills in the following menuet by Lully therefore should start with the main note or perhaps with a very light upper note.

Example 1 'Lully's Trills in a Menuet'

Lully. Menuet from *Amadis* (1684)

Most of the notes bearing main-note trills in Rousseau's viol tutor are approached melodically from below or decorate short notes. Rousseau says that the trill in the seventh measure of Example 2 may be started with the upper note if the upper note is played very lightly. The other trills in the example are begun with the main note. Example 2 is not actually a dance piece, but similar passages occur in dance music. For the penultimate measure of this example, Rousseau says that the trill is shaken only during the second half of the note.

Example 2 'Rousseau's Trills with Main-note Start'

J. Rousseau. *Traité de la viole* (1687)

Most of Lully's trills that begin with the upper note are probably grace-note trills, that is, the initial upper-note precedes the time of the note bearing the trill sign. Rousseau in his vocal tutor (p. 54) says that the upper-note start takes its time from the previous note unless the main note is at least twice as long as the previous note, and preferably even longer. Rousseau's example in his viol tutor (pp. 78-79) shows the first five of eight trills to be grace-note trills and the last three to be trills with appoggiatura support, that is, these last three begin with an initial upper note that is played on the beat and held.

Example 3 'Rousseau's Realization of Trills with Upper-note Start'

J. Rousseau. *Traité de la viole* (1687)

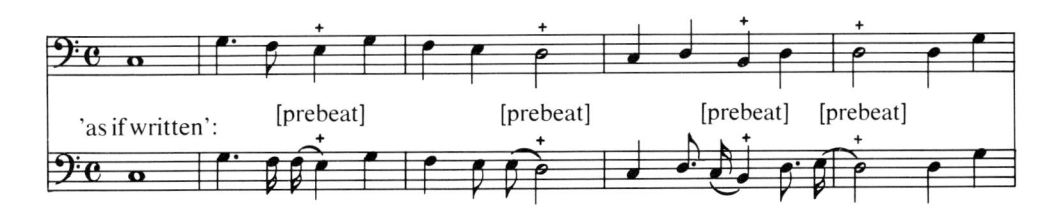

For trills with a two-note suffix, Lully writes the suffix in large notes. Notes bearing these trills usually ascend to the next note. Though the scores do not show the trilled note and suffix to be slurred, they probably should be in performance.

Example 4 'Lully's Notation of Trills with a Two-note Suffix'

Lully. Menuet from *Roland* (1685)

A trill with appoggiatura support appears at the end of the double for the minuet song, 'Est-on sage,' in Lully's opera *Psyché* of 1678. However, because *Psyché* was not published until 1720, and no manuscript exists, the double may not be by Lully. In any case, the complete ornament — appoggiatura support, alternations and one-note suffix — last for the duration of a half note. Interestingly, the appoggiatura support is notated as half the value of the complete ornament. Nevertheless, all or some of the alternations may perhaps anticipate the note marked with the trill sign (as in the fully anticipated and straddling trills to be described shortly).

Example 5 'Supported-appoggiatura Trill in a Double to a Menuet by Lully'

Lully (?). Double of Menuet from *Psyché* (published 1720) (last two measures)

Trills in Concert Solos

Trills in concert solos are often more elaborate than those in pieces to accompany actual dancing. Many dance pieces for solo harpsichord or lute, or for viola da gamba or flute accompanied by basso continuo, include a great profusion and variety of ornaments. Indeed, French composers of the late 17th and early 18th centuries were celebrated for their care in specifying ornamentation in solos for concert use. And some concert solos give information that is rich in details of performance. The composers of *airs de cour* and of keyboard solos were the most meticulous in designating the various performances of trills.

The use of only one or two signs for all trills in a concert solo does not mean that each of these signs specifies a single execution. Rather, modern wind and string players should study the carefully notated ornaments in *airs de cour* and in keyboard dances to find the forms used and the places most appropriate for every form.

D'Anglebert's harpsichord pieces of 1689[6] are especially helpful in showing the performance of trills in dance music. His Table of Ornaments includes seven kinds of trill, a substitute for a trill, and a 'detachment,' or articulation silence, before a trill. Each manner of execution has a particular sign, and these signs appear in suitable places in the dances of the collection.

Example 6 'D'Anglebert's Trills'

a) *tremblement simple*
   (simple trill)

b) *tremblement appuyé*
   (appoggiatura-
   supported trill)

c) *cadence*
   (descending
   cadential trill)

d) *autre [cadence]*
   (ascending
   cadential trill)

e) *double cadence*
   (downward plus upward slide
   plus ascending cadential trill)

f) *autre [double cadence]*
   (downward plus upward
   slide plus descending
   cadential trill)

g) *sans tremblement*
   (turn instead of
   a trill)

h) *tremblement
   et pincé*
   (trill with
   2-note suffix)

i) *détaché avant
   un tremblement*
   (articulation
   silence before
   a trill)

There is not space in this article to discuss in depth D'Anglebert's use of trills. However, readers who study his pieces of 1689 will find that on long notes he chiefly used the appoggiatura-supported trill and at cadences, the several compound trills that he calls *cadences* and *doubles cadences*. He mainly used trills and mordents on short notes. Example 7 shows the opening measures of a courante by D'Anglebert. The wealth of information given there is also characteristic of his other pieces, including some transcriptions of dances by Lully.

Example 7 'Ornaments in a Courante by D'Anglebert'

D'Anglebert. Courante (1689)

The rest sign over the initial upbeat note in Example 7 shows that a detachment, or articulation silence, precedes the following trill. The alternations of that trill may be accelerated after the appoggiatura support. Whether accelerated or not, such a trill may be anchored on the upper note. That is, the appoggiatura may be emphasized through the trilling. The alternations then come to a halt, or rest point, on the dot of the note. The simple trill on the downbeat of the second measure should probably be performed as a main-note trill — or perhaps as a grace-note trill, a fully-anticipated trill or a straddling trill with a rest point on the main note — in order that the main-note F♯ rather than the upper-note G be heard as the second voice.

When the trilled note is a quarter note preceded by another quarter note in 3, 2, 6/4 or ₵ meters — or an eighth note preceded by an eighth note in 3/8 or 6/8 meters — the relative brevity of the note under the trill sign suggests that all or some of the alternations may take place in the time of the previous note. The trill then concludes with a rest point on the pitch of the main note. These are the fully anticipated and the straddling trills. A fully anticipated performance is implied for two of the trills in François Couperin's Table of Ornaments in his first book of harpsichord pieces (1713).[7] If the starts of the notes line up as Couperin has notated them, the alternations precede the note marked with the trill sign. If instead only a few of the alternations begin early, and some continue into the time of the note under the trill sign, the alternations straddle the two notes. In both cases, the prebeat alternations may be anchored on the upper or the main note.

Example 8 'François Couperin's Prebeat Trills'

F. Couperin. 'Explication des agréments, et des signes,' *Premier livre de pièces de clavecin* (1713)

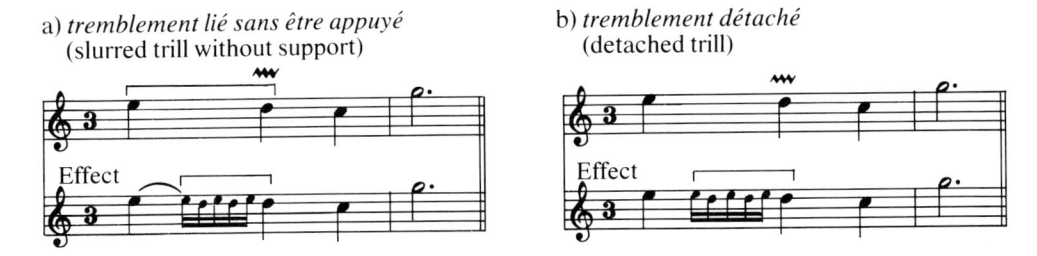

a) *tremblement lié sans être appuyé*
(slurred trill without support)

b) *tremblement détaché*
(detached trill)

Other versions of the trill are given in ornamentation tables by other composers. And more ornate versions are sometimes written in large or small notes in slow dance pieces and in doubles. For instance, Hotteterre's sarabande 'La fidelle', Op. 2/2 has a number of ornamented trills.

Example 9 'Ornamented Trills in a Sarabande by Hotteterre'

Hotteterre. Sarabande 'La fidelle', Op. 2/2 (1707)

Any delay of the main-note-anchored alternations of a trill breaks the musical flow. My colleague at the University of Iowa, harpsichordist and musicologist Sven Hansell, discusses in an article[8] and in work currently in progress the effect of prebeat and onbeat ornaments on the forward motion of passages. Although he is chiefly studying harpsichord music, his findings work equally in music for voice and other instruments. Hansell argues that the principal importance of harpsichord ornaments is not to sustain notes — as so often claimed — but to aid or interrupt the flow toward the cadence. He thus prefers prebeat ornaments for most music in which the *notes inégales* move in bad-good pairs. That is, the second of two eighth notes making up a quarter note in 3, 2, 6/4 or ¢ meter is grouped with the first eighth note of the following quarter note, as by the woodwind syllables *tu-ru*. This bad-good grouping prevails in French dances. But Hansell points out that onbeat ornaments in this music are useful at a repose or to break the flow just before it: a shift from bad-good pairs to good-bad pairs produces a brief interruption in the forward motion.

Hansell also prefers onbeat trills for passages with good-bad pairs of notes. The good-bad pairing subtly accents the good notes and must therefore be aided by ornaments with onbeat starts, which also make accents. In other words, Hansell shows that most passages with bad-good grouping of the notes favor prebeat trills, that most passages with good-bad grouping favor onbeat trills, and that the most arresting notes in hemiolas and at other types of cadences use onbeat ornaments to delay the alternations anchored on the main note. A turn or other embellished start of a compound trill, as in D'Anglebert's two *cadences* and two *doubles cadences* in c), d), e), f) of Example 6, also delay the start of the alternations and thereby increase the need for, or impetus toward, the imminent repose.

Some composers, such as Boismortier, may limit the number of trill signs to two. Although Boismortier does not identify his signs, a short wavy line, or chevron, seems to indicate a simple trill. This ornament usually occurs over a relatively short note and thus must begin with the main note or with a very light auxiliary, and must often be started in the time of the previous note. This trill usually has time for only one or two alternations; the alternations may anticipate the beat and be followed by a rest point. The cross, or plus sign, instead appears over longer notes or over notes at cadences. Therefore this ornament seems to require a start with the upper note played long enough to be readily perceived. This trill has time for more than two alternations; the alternations probably continue throughout the duration of an undotted note and stop for a rest point on the dot of a dotted note. The initial auxiliary must be played as a grace note if the note under the cross is relatively short, but on the beat and with at least some support if the note is longer. The rondeau refrain of Boismortier's 'Bourrée en rondeau', from Opus 35/5, demonstrates both trill signs.

Example 10 'The Two Trill Signs in Boismortier's Flute Suites'

Boismortier. 'Bourrée en rondeau' from Suite V, Opus 35 (1731)

Coordinating Trills in Several Voices
Late 17th- and early 18th-century players of duets, trios and larger concerted pieces presumably did not have to sit down before reading a dance piece to decide how to perform its trills. Rather, a certain group of conventions was followed. And, in any case, the more players involved, the simpler the performance of the trills.

Duets and trios may include ornamented trills written by the composer. Or the players of the melody parts may improvise their own embellishments for the more important or longer trills. Main-note and prebeat starts facilitate clarity in many places in quick dances with two or three melodic parts. Even in François Couperin's courante in Example 11, marked 'noblement,' the simplest performance of the trills is the most melodious.

Example 11 'The Trills in a Measure of a Courante by F. Couperin'

F. Couperin. Courante from 'L'Espagnole', *Les Nations* (1726) (measure 3)

Noblement

For the trill on the fifth quarter note of the measure in Example 11, the top voice begins its trilling with the two prebeat notes indicated by Couperin, and the alternations continue with main-note anchor to the dot. The simplest performance of the trill in the second voice best suits the voice leading in the other two parts. If the trill is fully anticipated — that is, if its trilling takes place during the time of the previous note — the F-G-F in the second voice coincides with the first D-E$^\flat$-D of the trill in the top voice and the pitches of the two voices are harmonious, being a sixth apart. Moreover, this performance avoids parallel octaves between the alternations of the second voice and those of the bass, provided that the alternations in the bass begin on the beat as the notation implies. Couperin starts the bass trill with a slow slide (E$^\flat$-F) before the beat. The slow tempo of the slide suggests that the alternations begin on the beat and slowly, probably with the upper note (G). This slow initial upper note clashes momentarily with the main-note D in the top voice, adding spice to the cadence. The alternations continue in the bass with some acceleration, probably until the two-note suffix written by Couperin.

If the two upper-voice trills on the downbeat of the following measure are performed as grace-note trills, the initial auxiliary coincides approximately with the F in the bass. The auxiliary is slurred to its main note, which follows it, whereas the F in the bass is slurred to its previous notes; this discrepancy of attacks adds spice to the cadence. More spice can be added by delaying the auxiliary until the downbeat. Still more spice results from holding the onbeat auxiliary before starting the alternations. And a different kind of spice is given by compound trills such as D'Anglebert's *cadences* and *doubles cadences* in Example 6. At a cadence, the performer's taste — like that of a fine chef — determines the kind and the proper amount of spice.

The trills in the dances of orchestral suites must be given the simplest possible performance. Then, as long as the rhythmic 'swing' of the dance is felt similarly by all players, the trills will fall naturally into place. For greater expression, the soloist in an orchestral suite can further embellish his trills, even when they coincide with simpler performance by the other players. Slow and expressive dances in orchestral suites as elsewhere allow the greatest variety of trill performance.

This article has shown that clarity and an understanding of a trill's function are the important factors in determining the performance of a trill. But, after studying and playing the numerous trill executions specified by Jean Rousseau, D'Anglebert, Hotteterre, François Couperin,

Boismortier and numerous other composers, a performer can rely on his intuition — an intuition based on experience, knowledge and sensitivity — to guide him. At that point most trills will 'come out right' without forethought. As expressed by Saint-Lambert in the quotation that heads this article, good taste is then the only law.[9]

Notes

1 Saint-Lambert, Michel de. *Les principes du clavecin*. Paris, 1702. Facsimile, Geneva: Minkoff, 1974.

2 Neumann, Frederick. *Ornamentation in Baroque and Post-Baroque Music: With Special Emphasis on J.S. Bach*. Princeton: Princeton University Press, 1978.

3 Rousseau, Jean. *Méthode clair, certaine et facile, pour apprendre à chanter la musique*. Paris, 1678.

4 Rousseau, Jean. *Traité de la viole*. Paris, 1687. Facsimile, Amsterdam: Antiqua, 1965.

5 Borjon, Charles Emmanuel. *Traité de la musette, avec une nouvelle méthode, pour apprendre de soy-mesme à jouer de cet instrument facilement, & en peu de temps*. Lyon, 1672.

6 Anglebert, Jean-Henry d'. *Pièces de clavecin. Paris,* 1689. Ed. Kenneth Gilbert. Le Pupitre IIV. Paris: Heugel, 1975.

7 *Couperin, François. Pièces de clavecin. Premier Livre*. Paris, 1713. Ed. Kenneth Gilbert. Le Pupitre XXI. Paris: Heugel, 1972.

8 Hansell, Sven H. 'Folk Fiddling in Sweden: Ornamentation and Irregular Rhythm and its Relation to Seventeenth-Century French Keyboard Music'. Unpublished paper read at Annual Meeting, American Musicological Society, Denver, Colorado, 8 November 1980.

9 The material for this article comes from a book, *The Interpretation of French Baroque Dance Music*, being written by Betty Bang Mather and Dean Karns.

Copyright © 1984 by Betty Bang Mather

A new look at the life of John Loeillet (1680-1730)

David Lasocki

John Loeillet holds an important place in the history of the flute in England.[1] He was the first musician of stature to play the Baroque flute in his adopted country, and probably the first composer to publish idiomatic chamber music for the instrument there. The biographies of the members of the Loeillet family have been the subject of much confusion in the literature, especially in the writings of Bergmans and Closson early this century. But most of this confusion was cleared up by Brian Priestman and Alec Skempton in the 1950s and 60s.[2] Recently Morag Deane has published some new information on the family, unfortunately containing many errors,[3] and the distinction scholars have made between John Loeillet of London and Jean-Baptiste Loeillet of Ghent has been questioned, without any new evidence being introduced, by Rose-Marie Janzen.[4] The present article re-examines John Loeillet's life on the basis of all the available evidence, some of which has not previously been cited in the literature on the family.

John Loeillet, the son of Jean Baptiste François Loeillet (1653-1685), a surgeon, and his second wife Barbe (née Buys), was born in Ghent and baptised 'Jean-Baptiste' at the St. Jacobskerk there on 18 November 1680.[5] His brother Jacob (Jacques), who also became a celebrated woodwind player, was born in 1685.[6] After their father's death in 1685, the two brothers may have been brought up by their uncle, Pierre Loeillet I (1651-1735), a violinist and concertmaster in Ghent and the father of the other Jean-Baptiste Loeillet (1688-1715), often called 'de Gant' to distinguish him from his cousin.[7]

Nothing certain is known of John's early life and training. Deane has speculated that he was driven from his native Ghent by the French occupation of The Netherlands during the War of the Spanish Succession.[8] He had certainly arrived in London by 10 April 1705 when, along with James Paisible,[9] John Banister II,[10] and other members of the Drury Lane Theatre band, he performed 'a piece of instrumental music' in the intermission of a play.[11] This evidence suggests that he had become a member of that band, almost certainly as an oboist – a place he was to hold in another theatre band within three years (that of the Queen's Theatre; see below). The first oboe at Drury Lane at that time was Peter La Tour, a Frenchman who seems to have arrived in England in the last decade of the seventeenth century.[12] Whether La Tour remained first oboe and Loeillet played second oboe, or whether Loeillet's superior talent was immediately rewarded with the first oboe place is a matter for speculation, since no personnel rosters for Drury Lane seem to have survived. We do know that the two oboists would have been employed in the band in the dramatic music for plays and accompaniments for operas, and would have occasionally played chamber music in the entertainments given in the intermissions between the acts of the plays.

On 12 February 1706, in a concert at York Buildings, the instrumental music included 'several entertainments upon the German flute (never performed before) by Mr. Latour.'[13] The Baroque transverse flute – usually called the 'German flute' in England in the first half of the eighteenth century – was performed in London in 1702 and seems to have been known even in the 1690s.[14] The concert of La Tour's is, however, the first reference to the instrument in newspaper advertisements.[15] The 'never performed before' tag may have been intended to refer only to the concerts at York Buildings or, more likely, was an advertising ploy by promoters hoping that this instrument was still rare enough to be novel for most of the audience.

It is commonly stated that John Loeillet was responsible for introducing the transverse flute to England in 1705. He clearly did not introduce it, nor was he the first advertised performer on the instrument. The question now arises: did La Tour either already know how to play the flute when he arrived in England from France (a country where flute playing was already well established) or learn the instrument after arriving in England from a player such as Paisible or François La Riche (who were supposed to have provided the flute tablature for the Talbot manuscript)? If so, one would have expected him to have shown it off in public before the vaunted concert debut in 1706. In view of the date of this debut – the year after Loeillet arrived in the country – it seems much more likely to me that it was in fact Loeillet who taught La Tour how to play the instrument (or at least, to play it proficiently enough to use in public concerts). In any case, La Tour played the flute in two other advertised public concerts during the next two years,[16] and the year after that, 1709, the instrument was played in another public concert by Humphrey Denby, a colleague of La Tour's in the oboe band of Queen Anne and Prince George of Denmark.[17] In other words, the leading oboists in England began to teach each other to play the new instrument. The question still remains, however, as to why, if Loeillet was the player who first demonstrated the artistic potential of the new instrument, it was not he but La Tour who introduced the instrument in the London concerts. The answer may perhaps lie in Loeillet's generous personality (see below): he taught his colleague the instrument and allowed him the pleasure of its first concert performance.

To return to the work of Loeillet and La Tour in the Drury Lane band, in 1706 and 1707 the company put on revivals of three dramatic works with music by Henry Purcell including both recorder and oboe parts: *Bonduca* ('with all the original music'), *The Indian Queen*, and *Timon of Athens*.[18] On 1 April 1707, *Thomyris, Queen of Scythia*, adapted by Heidegger from works by Alessandro Scarlatti, Bononcini and Steffani, began a long run at Drury Lane.[19] It has, besides parts for two oboes, an aria, 'Cares on a crown', with transverse flute obbligato, and another, 'Pretty Warbler', with recorder obbligato, both of which were presumably written for either La Tour or Loeillet.[20]

Loeillet probably played in concerts with other members of the band during the next few years, although the only advertisement in which he is mentioned by name is for a concert at York Buildings 'with sonatas on several instruments' by him, Paisible, Banister, and the harpsichordist Francis Dieupart (by that time also a member of the Drury Lane band) on 23 May 1707.[21] Loeillet probably played the oboe (and/or flute and recorder), Paisible the recorder, and Banister the recorder and/or violin in this concert. We may also assume that either Loeillet or La Tour was the flautist for whom William Corbett wrote a part in his 1708 publication, *Six Sonatas with an Overture and Aires in four parts for a Trumpet, Violin's and Hautboys, Flute de Allmain, Bassoons or harpsichord*,[22] which were probably the 'several new pieces for trumpets and flutes, composed by Mr. Corbett' that were performed in a concert at York Buildings on 26 March 1707.[23]

Around November 1707 Loeillet is named as first oboe at 15s per night (La Tour was second

oboe) in the list of prospective musicians for the production of operas at the Queen's Theatre.[24] In the tentative roster for that theatre made around early December, he is listed as the first of four oboes at £ 40 per annum, the highest salary level of the rank-and-file members.[25]
In December he was one of the Drury Lane instrumentalists given permission to rehearse an opera secretly at the Queen's Theatre and dismissed for their action by Christopher Rich, the Drury Lane manager.[26] He appears in the musicians' petition for reinstatement at Drury Lane, although the amount he had been earning there, unlike those of the other musicians dismissed, is not stated.[27] In the estimate of charges for the opera productions made in January 1708, he is again listed first of two oboes (with La Tour) at 15s per night.[28] When production did start on the 13th of that month, he and La Tour were hired as first and second oboes, respectively, Loeillet at the fee that had been estimated.[29]

A concert announced for York Buildings on January 21st was to have included 'a full piece of the famous Signior Bononcini [performed] by Mr. Dean Sen., Mr. Beeston, and Mr. Luly [sic] &c.'; the wording of the advertisement suggests that the piece was a trio sonata for two violins and basso continuo, performed with more than one player to a part, in which Loeillet played the harpsichord.[30] But the concert was postponed to Stationers Hall on 4 February, when the piece in which Loeillet was to have played was replaced in the advertisement and presumably he did not perform after all.[31]

Some of the operas performed at the Queen's during this period contain significant wind parts. *Love's Triumph*, adapted by Valentini Urbani from Gasparini and Cesarini, was first performed on 26 February 1708.[32] It contains several arias with oboe parts; one, 'If ever 'tis my', with recorders doubling the violins; and another, 'You're so pretty', with recorder obbligato.[33] *Pyrrhus and Demetrius* (14 December 1708), adapted by Haym from A. Scarlatti, has only oboe parts.[34] *Clotilda* (2 March 1709),[35] adapted by Heidegger from Conti, Scarlatti and Bononcini, has an aria with oboe obbligato and another, 'Cares when they're over', with an obbligato for a 'small flute [recorder]', apparently the first documented music for such an instrument in England at this time.[36] All these parts would have been performed by the oboists – Loeillet and La Tour – doubling on flute and recorder as the occasion demanded (although Paisible and Banister may occasionally have taken some of the recorder parts).

In 1709 the anonymous translator (Nicola Francesco Haym?) of l'Abbé François Raguenet's *A Comparison between the French and Italian Musick and Opera's* says that 'Mr. Lulliet' as an oboist 'need not give place to any [Master] at Paris'.[37] His recorder playing, unlike that of Paisible and Banister, is not mentioned. Neither is his flute playing (although the instrument may not have been established long enough yet to merit attention). The translator does, however, describe Loeillet's harpsichord playing as 'inferior to few in Italy'.[38] Another testament to his harpsichord playing is his *Lessons for the harpsichord or spinet, viz. almands, corants, sarabands, airs, minuets & jiggs*, which Daniel Wright published around 1709 to 1715. (The composer is listed as 'Mr. Baptist Lully', typical of the confusion that surrounded Loeillet's name in England, although here perhaps used intentionally to create more sales by making the public believe they were buying music by the celebrated seventeenth-century French opera composer Jean-Baptiste Lully.) Sir John Hawkins called Loeillet both 'a celebrated master of the harpsichord' and a 'teacher of the harpsichord'.[39]

The most important event for the Queen's at this period, and indeed for music in England in general, was the arrival of Handel in London for the first time in 1710. On 24 February 1711, his *Rinaldo* was produced at the Queen's to enormous success.[40] It includes the celebrated aria

'Augelletti', which has parts for 'flauto piccolo' and two alto recorders, performed from behind the scenes to represent the song of the live birds that were released on the stage (who presumably could not themselves be relied upon to sing at the right time).[41] Loeillet and La Tour presumably played the two alto recorder parts in this aria (the 'flauto piccolo' part may well have been performed by Banister or Paisible). Loeillet remained first oboe of the band at the Queen's Theatre until the 1710-11 season,[42] but he seems to have left the band by the end of that season, since he is not mentioned in a wage list made during the 1711-12 season that apparently names those musicians from the 1709-10 season still with the band.[43]

Presumably Loeillet had begun to make an independent living from teaching and giving private concerts. Hawkins says that Loeillet,
dwelling in a house in Hart Street, Covent Garden, in which was a large room, had a weekly concert there, which was frequented chiefly by gentlemen performers, who gratified him very handsomely for his assistance in conducting it.[44]
These concerts were never advertised in the newspapers, so we do not know the music performed there (with one exception) or the professional performers besides Loeillet (if any). But Hawkins relates what happened at a concert on one famous occasion, presumably at the end of 1714 or beginning of 1715.[45] Henry Needler – Accountant-General of the Excise, a keen amateur violinist, on which instrument he was a pupil of Banister, and a noted admirer and performer of Corelli's works – 'was used to frequent' Loeillet's concerts.

There lived at that time opposite Southampton Street, in the Strand, where Mr. Elmsley now resides, Mr. Prevost, a bookseller, who dealt largely to Holland. It happened that one day he had received a large consignment of books from Amsterdam, and among them the concertos [Opus 6] of Corelli, which had just then been published; upon looking at them he thought of Mr. Needler, and immediately went with them to his house in Clement's Lane, behind St. Clement's church in the Strand, but being informed that Mr. Needler was then at the concert of Mr. Loeillet's, he went with them thither. Mr. Needler was transported with the sight of such a treasure; the books were immediately laid out, and he and the rest of the performers played the whole twelve concertos through, without rising from their seats.[46]

Loeillet's only other documented performance after he left the Queen's Theatre is as an oboist in a pair of private concerts at the Kensington home of the Duchess of Shrewsbury, the wife of the Lord Chamberlain, around 1712-13, for which he received the sum of £ 8.[47] (Loeillet and the two principal violins had the highest fees of the instrumentalists.) On 15 December 1712, the Vice-Chamberlain paid Loeillet the sum of eight guineas, the reason for which is unknown.[48] The receipt, which is probably a holograph, is signed 'J: Loeillet'.

Loeillet contributed four dances to a collection published by the choreographer Kellom Tomlinson around 1720 under the title *Six Danses ... being a collection of all the yearly dances published by him from the year 1715 to the present day*. The third of them is known to have been danced at Lincoln's Inn Fields Theatre on 21 February 1717 by the young French brother and sister team of Salle (first name unknown) and his sister Marie.[49] Tomlinson was presumably one of the regular choreographers for that theatre – a 'scholar' of his danced there between 1716 and 1718 – so the other three dances of Loeillet's may well have been performed there in 1715, 1716 and 1718.

In 1720 Loeillet was considered for the post of first oboist in the opera orchestra of the new Royal Academy of Music at a salary of £ 60, but his name was cancelled in favor of 'Joseph' (probably Joseph Woodbridge).[50] In 1722 Loeillet, along with Raphael Courteville and the distinguished keyboard players George Frideric Handel, William Babell and William Croft, was employed to test a new organ at St. Dionis Backchurch.[51] In 1726 and 1727 he was one of the subscribers to the Academy of Ancient Music, which met at the Crown and Anchor Tavern in the Strand.[52] He was also one of the subscribers (in the other sense of the word) to the published scores of Handel's operas *Rodelinda* (1725) and *Alessandro* (1726).[53]

Loeillet's character, convivial and self-effacing, is portrayed in the poem 'The Session of Musicians' (in imitation of Sir John Suckling's 'The Session of the Poets', 1637), published in 1724, which recounts Apollo's attempt to award a prize to the best musician in England.[54]

Apollo's piercing eye just then espied
Merry L[oe]i[l]l[e]t stand laughing at one side;
He gently waved him to him with his hand,
Wond'ring he at that distance chose to stand.
Smiling, he said, I come not here for fame,
Nor do I to the bays pretend a claim;
Few here deserve so well, the god replied,
But modesty does always merit hide;
A supper for some friends I've just bespoke,
Pray come — and drink your glass — and crack your joke.

During the 1720s, Walsh & Hare published four major collections of Loeillet's compositions. Opus 1 (1722) comprised three trio sonatas for alto recorder, oboe or violin, and basso continuo, and three for two flutes and basso continuo. Six suites for harpsichord came out in 1723. Opus 2 (*ca.* 1725) consisted of six trio sonatas for two violins and basso continuo, three for alto recorder, oboe and basso continuo, and three for two flutes and basso continuo. Opus 3 (1729) comprised six sonatas for alto recorder and basso continuo, and six for flute and basso continuo.[55] These compositions, mostly for Loeillet's own instruments – harpsichord, oboe, recorder, and flute – presumably summarize his own contribution to his concert series over the years. Opus 2 was dedicated to 'the most Illustrious Prince John, Duke of Rutland, one of the Lords of His Majesty's Bedchamber' and Opus 3 to 'Charles Edwin, Esq.' – perhaps two of the gentlemen who patronized Loeillet's concerts.

By 1729, Loeillet had moved from Hart Street.[56] The notice of his death, printed on 25 July 1730 in *Fog's Weekly Journal*, states:

on Sunday [that is, 19 July] in the evening died at his house in East Street near Red Lion Square, Mr. Lullie, after a short indisposition. He was an excellent Master of music, and died much regretted by all that were acquainted with him.[57]

This address is confirmed by another newspaper advertisement quoted below. (Hawkins gives an address round the corner: 'In the latter part of his life he dwelt in New North Street, near Red Lion Square'.)[58] No record of his burial is to be found in the parish registers of St. George the Martyr, or of any other London parish that I have been able to conceive as a possible resting place. Perhaps his body was taken back to The Netherlands.

Loeillet's will was drawn up on 1 May 1729, suggesting that perhaps his indisposition was not as short as the newspaper claimed.[59] Loeillet names his brother Jacques among the beneficiaries and his uncle Pierre as residuary legatee. The legacies add up to £ 1,700 and the residue of the estate could have been far more. (Hawkins claims that Loeillet 'by his industry acquired a fortune of £ 16,000'.)[60] The will shows him to have been rich enough to afford several domestic servants (Paisible had only one). The instruments mentioned are 'the very best of my harpsichords' (implying that he had several) and 'violins, flutes of all kinds, bass violins'. Did he also play members of the violin family, or were those instruments only for the use of his gentlemen concertizers? The year after his death a newspaper advertisement announced:

To be auctioned on 18 May. The entire household goods of Mr. John Loeillet, professor of musick, deceased; furniture, pictures, particularly a very excellent drawing of the Last Supper by Raphael, two harpsichords, spinets and other musical instruments of the finest workmanship ... and jewels and plate. Which may be seen at his late dwelling house in East Street near Red Lion Square. Catalogues at the house and at Mr. Cook's in Bread Street near Golden Square.[61]

Notes

1 This article is an expanded version of a section of a chapter in my recent study, *Professional Recorder Players in England, 1540-1740*, 2 vols. (Ph.D. dissertation, The University of Iowa, 1983), II, 875-82. I would like to thank Robert D. Hume (University Park, Pennsylvania), Judith Milhous (Iowa City, Iowa), and Maurice Byrne (Leamington, Warwickshire) for drawing my attention to some of the documents cited.

2 Brian Priestman, 'Catalogue thématique des oeuvres de Jean-Baptiste, John & Jacques Loeillet', *Revue Belge de Musicologie* VI (1952), 219-74; *ibid.*, 'An Introduction to the Loeillets', *The Consort* XI (1954), 18-26; *ibid.*, 'The Keyboard Works of John Loeillet', *Music Review* XVI (1955), 89-95; *ibid.*, 'Loeillet', *Die Musik in Geschichte und Gegenwart* VIII (1960), cols. 1100-04; Alec Skempton, 'The Instrumental Sonatas of the Loeillets', *Music & Letters* XLIII (1962), 206-17. Their findings are summarized in Alec Skempton & Lucy Robinson, 'Loeillet', *The New Grove* XI, 124-26.

3 'John Loeillet of London', *Recorder & Music* VI/8 (December 1979), 226-29; 'Jacob Loeillet and Jean Baptiste Loeillet de Gand', *Recorder & Music* VI/10 (June 1980), 286-88.

4 'Die Identität von Jean-Baptiste Loeillet', *Tibia* 1/82, 1-6.

5 Priestman, 'An Introduction to the Loeillets', 18-19.

6 Skempton, *op. cit.*, 210.

7 Jean-Baptiste's year of death is taken from Deane, 'Jacob Loeillet and Jean Baptiste Loeillet', 288.

8 'John Loeillet of London', 227.

9 For Paisible's life, see Lasocki, *op. cit.*, II, 789-815.

10 For Banister's life, see Lasocki, *op. cit.*, II, 816-29.

11 Emmett L. Avery, ed., *The London Stage, 1660-1800. Part II: 1700-1729*, 2 vols. (Carbondale: Southern Illinois University Press, 1960) [hereinafter abbreviated as 'LS'], I, 91; Michael Tilmouth, 'A Calendar of References to Music in Newspapers published in London and the Provinces (1660-1719)', *Royal Musical Association Research Chronicle* I (1960) [hereinafter abbreviated as 'TC'], 60.

12 For La Tour's life, see Lasocki, *op. cit.*, II, 870-75.

13 LS II/1, 117.

14 A flute by Bressan is described in James Talbot's manuscript, compiled between 1695 and 1701. (On this manuscript see Anthony Baines, 'James Talbot's Manuscript [Christ Church Library Music MS 1187]. 1. Wind Instruments', *Galpin Society Journal* I [1948] 9-26. For further information on the dating of the manuscript, see Lasocki, *op. cit.*, I, 518, n. 9.) An aria 'Hither turn thee, gentle swain', with 'Flute D.Almagne', two violins and basso continuo, which appears in John Eccles' setting of Congreve's *The Judgment of Paris* for the prize competition at Dorset Garden Theatre in 1701, seems to have been the first published flute music in England. It certainly antedates by ten years an aria in Galliard's *Calypso and Telemachus* (Queen's Theatre, 14 May 1712), which Roger Fiske (*English Theatre Music in the Eighteenth Century* [London: Oxford University Press, 1973], 55) singles out for the honour of being the first aria of the period with flute obbligato.

15 Such advertisements only began to mention the instruments featured in concerts and theatre intermission entertainments with the publication of the first daily newspaper, the *Daily Courant*, in 1702. But it is worth noting that the flute is not mentioned in the advertisements between 1702 and 1706, and in any case, La Tour's performance is heralded as a debut.

16 LS II/1, 146; TC, 68, 71.

17 LS II/1, 198; TC, 74. For Denby's life, see Lasocki, *op. cit.*, II, 955-56.

18 LS II/1, 112, 117, 118, 122, 126, 127, 135, 138.

19 LS II/1, 144.

20 *Songs in the New Opera Call'd Thomyris . . . Contriv'd so that their Symphonys may be perform'd with them* (London: Walsh, Hare & Randall, 1707).

21 LS II/1, 148; TC, 69.

22 Opus 3 (London: Walsh & Hare, 1708).

23 LS II/1, 144; TC, 68.

24 Judith Milhous & Robert D. Hume, *Vice-Chamberlain Coke's Theatrical Papers, 1706-1715* (Carbondale & Edwardsville: Southern Illinois University Press, 1982) [hereinafter abbreviated as *Coke Papers*], 31. He is not found in the attached petition.

25 With La Tour, (William?) Smith and an unnamed fourth oboist (*ibid.*, 33). In a similar list made in late December, he is the first of four oboes (with Smith, La Tour and Roussellett) at the same salary (*ibid.*, 38).

26 *Ibid.*, 31.

27 *Ibid.*, 47. This petition confirms Loeillet's employment at Drury Lane.

28 *Ibid.*, 69.

29 *Ibid.*, 70.

30 TC, 70.

31 TC, 71; LS II/1, 165.

32 LS II/1, 167. It received seven more performances that season but was never produced again.

33 *The Symphonys or Instrumental Parts in the Opera Call'd Love's Triumph* (London: Walsh & Hare, 1708).

34 *Symphonys or Instrumental Parts in the Opera Call'd Pyrrhus and Demetrius* (London: Walsh & Hare, 1709); LS II/1, 180.

35 LS II/1, 186. It had six more performances that month and three in May 1711.

36 *The Symphonys or Instrumental Parts in the Opera Call'd Clotilda* (London: Walsh & Hare, 1709).

37 (London, 1709), 9n.

38 *Ibid.*, 52n-53n.

39 *A General History of the Science and Practice of Music* (London, 1776); ed. Charles Cudworth, 2 vols. (New York: Dover, 1963), II, 823.

40 LS II/1, 243.

41 See the descriptions of the scene by John Addison and Sir Richard Steele in *The Spectator*, 6 and 16 March 1711, both conveniently reproduced in Otto Erich Deutsch, *Handel: A Documentary Biography* (London: Adam & Charles Black, 1955), 35-37.

42 Lists of band personnel, season of 1708-09, 15s per night (*Coke Papers*, 118); season of 1709-10 (*ibid.*, 127); season of 1710-11 (*ibid.*, 151); late November 1710 (*ibid.*, 158); December 1710 (*ibid.*, 159).

43 *Ibid.*, 179.

44 *Loc. cit.*

45 Corelli's concertos were advertised by Roger's London agent, Henry Ribboteau, on 1 January 1715. See François Lesure, *Bibliographie des éditions musicales publiées par Estienne Roger et Michel-Charles le Cène (Amsterdam, 1696-1743)* (Paris: Société Française de Musicologie/Heugel, 1969), 52.

46 *Ibid.*, II, 806.

47 *Coke Papers*, 191-92.

48 *Ibid.*, 194.

49 LS II/1, 437.

50 Judith Milhous & Robert D. Hume, 'New Light on Handel and the Royal Academy of Music in 1720', *Theatre Journal* XXXV/2 (May 1983), 158-60. For Woodbridge's life, see Lasocki, *op. cit.*, II, 961-62.

51 F.G. Edwards, 'Dr Charles Burney (1726-1814). A Biographical Sketch', *Musical Times* XLV/7 (No. 737) (July 1904), 435-36.

52 See the accounts of the Academy in British Library, Add. Ms. 11,732, ff. 3, 4.

53 Deutsch, *op. cit.*, 181, 196.

54 *Ibid.*, 167.

55 For full bibliographic references, see William C. Smith & Charles Humphries, *A Bibliography of the Musical Works Published by the Firm of John Walsh during the Years 1721-1766* (London: Bibliographical Society, 1968), Nos. 956-65.

56 He is not found in the rate books (the surviving volumes of which begin that year) for the parish of St. George the Martyr, Queen Square (Scavengers rate books in the possession of the Local History Library, Camden Borough Public Libraries). The 'John Leithieullier, Esq.' on the south side of Red Lion Square (the third house from Fisher Street and the thirteenth from Gray's Inn Passage) is presumably the father of Smart Lethieullier, the famous antiquary.

57 Quoted in Skempton, *op. cit.*, 209.

58 *Op. cit.*, II, 823.

59 The will is transcribed in Skempton, *op. cit.*, 216-17, and Deane, 'John Loeillet of London', 229.

60 *Loc. cit.*

61 *Daily Journal*, 11 May 1731.

Copyright © 1983 by David Lasocki

Die Flötenkonzerte von Pietro Nardini

Nikolaus Delius

Im Tagebuch einer musikalischen Reise des Doktors Charles Burney findet sich in dem Abschnitt über seinen Aufenthalt in Florenz (1770) folgender Eintrag (zitiert nach der deutschen Ausgabe Hamburg 1722): 'Montag, den 10ten Sept. Diesen Nachmittag hatte ich das Vergnügen, den Herrn Nardini und seinen kleinen Schüler, Linley, in einem Concerte, in eines Engländers, Herrn Hempsons Hause zu hören, wobey eine zahlreiche Gesellschaft war. Dieser Herr bläset die Flöttraverse auf eine besondere Art, indem er den Ton dadurch sehr verbessert, daß er in das Oberstück ein Stückchen Schwam anbringt, wodurch der Wind gehen muß. Er bließ ein paar schwere Concerte von Hasse und Nardini, und brachte sie recht gut heraus ...'
Als Komponist von Flötenwerken ist uns Nardini heute so gut wie unbekannt. Das dürfte auch zu früheren Zeiten nicht viel anders gewesen sein. Was die einschlägige Literatur dazu zu berichten weiß, hat Clara Pfäfflin in ihrer Dissertation zusammengetragen, die auch heute noch als die wesentliche Sekundärquelle angesprochen werden muß. (Pietro Nardini, seine Werke und sein Leben, Diss. 1930, Tübingen, 1935).
Das dort angefügte Werkverzeichnis nennt für bzw. mit Flöte lediglich die bei Bremner gestochenen 6 Sonaten für 2 Flöten oder Violinen und Baß, die überall zitiert werden, so auch von Vester im Flute Repertoire Catalogue (1967). Ebenso nennt Vester 6 Trios für 2 Flöten und Baß im Ms. (Mailand Cons.), das daraus in Neuausgabe erschienene Trio in C (Gümbel/Bärenreiter), ferner Trios für Flöte, Violine und Baß. Letztere Angabe geht vermutlich auf Schilling zurück, der aber eine gestochene Ausgabe und somit die Londoner von 1770 (Bremner) meinen muß.
So bleiben also die Angaben spärlich und darüberhinaus unzuverlässig. Bestätigt bleibt allerdings, daß Nardini im Zusammenhang mit der Flöte überwiegend Triosonaten komponiert hat, vermutlich etwa zwei Dutzend, die gestochene Londoner Ausgabe eingerechnet. Während Mather und Lasocki schon 1976 auf Verzierungen zu einem Adagio einer Sonate für Flöte und Baß, also eines 'Solo' aufmerksam machten (Free Ornamentation in Woodwind Music), weist auch McGowan in seiner Bibliographie *Italian Baroque Solo Sonatas*... 1978 noch kein einziges Werk Nardinis nach. Tatsächlich existieren aber Abschriften zweier Sonaten, zweier Duos für Flöten und zweier Konzerte außer den oben erwähnten Trios![1]
Es besteht sicher kein Zweifel, daß im Rahmen von Nardinis Gesamtschaffen die Violinwerke vorrangig zu betrachten sind, sowohl unter dem Gesichtspunkt der Kunst des Violinspiels wie unter dem der Verzierungskunst im ausgehenden 18. Jahrhundert. Daran ändert die Kenntnis der Flötenkompositionen nichts. Doch bleibt festzuhalten, daß ein so hervorragender Name, der bisher nur in Verbindung mit der Violine genannt wurde, eine ganze Reihe Kompositionen für die Flöte geliefert hat. Sie weisen allerdings keine flötenspezifischen Merkmale auf (außer der Beschränkung auf wenige gebräuchliche Tonarten), die nicht auch von den Violinwerken bekannt wären.
Die beiden überlieferten Konzerte stehen in G- und D-Dur. Es folgt hier eine Kurzbeschreibung von Annemarie Ehrle:[2]

Pietro Nardini

1. Konzert G-Dur

Incipit: Allegro

Anlage

harm. Schema   Motiveinh.   Längenverhältnisse der Soli

Allegro 4/4   Largo 3/8   Allegro 3/4

Tutti	T	A	B	C
Solo	T - D	A	D	C'
Tutti	D	A	B'	C''
Solo	D - Tp	A	D'	C'''
Tutti	Tp - T	A'	B	
Solo	T Kadenz	A''	D''	C''''
Tutti	T	A'''		C

Das harmonische Schema dieser Tabelle ist in allen drei Sätzen des Konzertes wieder zu finden. Auch der Beginn jedes Tutti und Solo mit der Motiveinheit A des Anfangstutti ist Prinzip aller drei Sätze, der weitere Verlauf ist variabel. Die Besetzung dieses Konzertes ist wie bei Tartini: 2 Violinen, Viola und Violoncello; ebenso besteht die Begleitung der Soli nur aus dem hellen Klang von zwei Violinen. Das Kopfmotiv und rhythmisch prägnante Stellen werden während des ganzen Konzertes meist in Terz- oder Sextparallelen geführt, im Solo übernimmt dabei die 1. Violine die Funktion der 2. Violine; die 2. Violine vertritt den Baß. In den virtuosen Soloepisoden tritt die Begleitung zurück in lange Notenwerte oder ruhig repetierende Achtelbewegung. Die dynamischen Bezeichnungen beschränken sich auf die Echogestaltung mit Forte und Piano. Durch die häufige Sequenz- und Fortspinnungsmanier, wie auch durch das neutrale ausgedehnte Passagenwesen steht das Konzert, trotz einiger stilistischer Merkmale neuerer Zeit, noch in barocker Tradition.

2. Konzert D-Dur

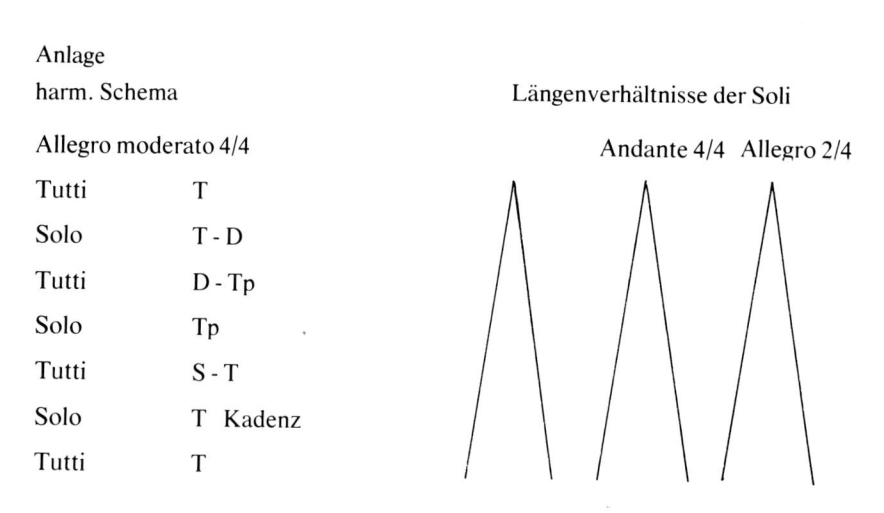

Incipit: Allegro moderato

Anlage

harm. Schema — Längenverhältnisse der Soli

Allegro moderato 4/4 — Andante 4/4   Allegro 2/4

Tutti	T
Solo	T - D
Tutti	D - Tp
Solo	Tp
Tutti	S - T
Solo	T Kadenz
Tutti	T

Die Tatsache, daß nun, im Vergleich zum G-Dur Konzert, bereits 'gemäßigtere' Tempobezeichnungen in den beiden ersten Sätzen verwendet wurden, läßt vielleicht auf ein anderes, späteres Entstehungsdatum schließen.

Aber auch die Anlage und Gestaltung des ganzen Konzertes ist etwas verändert, eine dreiteilige Form von Exposition, Durchführung und Reprise wird nun stärker erkennbar.

Die Melodik ist kleingliedriger, zäsurenreicher, fast immer werden die Pausen nun vom Baß überbrückt. Die viertaktige Periodik erscheint häufiger, wobei sich deutlich mehr oder weniger kontrastierende Einheiten, zum Teil auch auf der Dominante, voneinander abheben, entsprechend dem späteren zweiten Thema. Auch die motivische Arbeit gewinnt an Bedeutung, das neutrale Passagenwesen wird seltener, der Charakter einer Durchführung wird spürbar. Die dynamischen Bezeichnungen werden neben der Bezeichnung für das Echo als eigenständiges Gestaltungsmittel eingesetzt, das in schnellem Wechsel von piano und forte Kontraste auf kleinem Raum schafft. Auch der Stoß wird extra gekennzeichnet und bewußt angewandt.

Das Orchester besteht wiederum aus obligatem 'Streichquartett', in der Begleitung des Solos ist neben den Violinen auch das Cello beteiligt. Die Stimmen stehen in stärkerer Wechselbeziehung zueinander, oft imitatorischer Art oder als 'Untermalung' gehaltener Töne, sie zeigen ein lebhaftes Bild. Als Begleitstimmen treten sie aber auch in repetierende, trommelnde Sechzehntel oder ruhige Achtelbewegung zurück. Kadenzen sind hier ebenfalls gefordert, jedoch liegen sie nicht ausgeschrieben bei.

Bleibt zu fragen, was der Anlaß für so zahlreiche Flötenkompositionen Nardinis gewesen sein könnte. Eine Antwort läßt sich vielleicht bei Burney finden. Der o.g. Herr Hempson könnte Auftraggeber oder Adressat der Konzerte oder/und Sonaten gewesen sein. Ebensogut käme eine andere Möglichkeit in Betracht, nämlich die sicher enge Verbindung zu dem Flötisten Nicolas Dothel, von dem sich ebenfalls eine beachtliche Anzahl Kompositionen für Flöte in Genua befindet. Von ihm spricht Burney, wenig vor der oben zitierten Stelle:
'Obgleich Florenz itzt keinen Überfluß an musikalischen Genies hat, die es selbst hervorgebracht hätte, so ist es doch von anderen Orten recht gut damit versehen worden; denn außer den oben angeführten Sängern wohnt Sgr. Campioni als Kapellmeister des Großherzogs hier; Sgr. Dottel, ein berühmter Flötenspieler ist in der Kapelle, und Sgr. Nardini ist gleichfalls als erster Violinist in Großherzogl. Diensten.*

* ... Diese drey großen Meister ... wurden vor einiger Zeit durch die Freygebigkeit des Fürsten bewogen, Livorno zu verlassen.'

Anmerkungen

1 Genua, Cons. Neuausgabe demnächst bei Schott, Mainz.

2 Mit freundlicher Genehmigung der Autorin, die auf meine Anregung hin einige Flöten-Kompositionen Nardinis genauer untersucht hat und die Ergebnisse in einer Diplomarbeit in meiner Klasse an der Staatlichen Hochschule für Musik Freiburg 1984 vorgelegt hat.

John Gunn's 'The Art of Playing the German Flute on New Principles', London 1793.

'... How rarely a performer attains any higher excellence on his instrument than more rapidity ...'

Mirjam Nastasi

Die Überschrift dieses Aufsatzes, dem Vorwort der Flötenschule Gunn's entnommen, gibt in wenigen Worten wieder, was nicht nur im 18. Jahrhundert, sondern noch heute von manchem Instrumentalisten gesagt werden kann. Damals wie heute aber gibt es Musiker, die in Wort und Spiel Kritik an einer Art zu musizieren üben, bei der die Virtuosität im Vordergrund steht.

So hat auch der Flötist, Cellist, Pädagoge und Historiker John Gunn versucht, Mängel und Misstände offenzulegen, um damit seinem Instrument zu 'greater variety, expression and effect' zu verhelfen, wie es auf der Titelseite heisst.

Wie auffallend ähneln sich doch die Worte der Kritik von damals und heute! Ein Beispiel (Introduction, S. 1 - 2): 'Two opinions seem chiefly to prevail on the method in which this instrument ought to be played. The first is, that an equal fullness of tone ought to be aimed at throughout; and this, when required, is thought to be the greatest excellence of which the instrument is capable. The favourers of this opinion have on their side the example and practice of almost every public performer. The other opinion is in direct opposition to this, those ... say, that this kind of tone is contrary to the very nature of a Flute; the character of which, from its affinity to the female voice, is softness, grace and tender expression, and can by no means be the bold and warlike expression of those full and loud tones, which seem to emulate the notes of the trumpet ... I have often smiled at the conflict of these jarring opinions ... and have given little satisfaction to either party, by declaring ... that it was like asking a painter whether it were better for a picture to be all light or all shadow; ... yet the principle is an improper one to proceed upon, as it will only ... produce a monotony, the latter of these ... being less offensive, perhaps, because less noisy.'
Damit nimmt der Autor gleich zu Anfang seiner Schule Stellung zu einem für Flötisten bis heute aktuellen und kontroversen Thema.

John Gunn wurde etwa 1765 in Edinburgh geboren. Ausser Flötist war er auch Cellist und Verfasser einer Celloschule, welche kurz vor seinen beiden Flötenschulen erschien.[1] Ausserdem war er, wenn auch in bescheidenem Masse, Komponist.[2] Sein wissenschaftliches Interesse war vielseitig: ausser einem für diese Zeit ungewöhnlichen historischen Bewusstsein verfügte er auch über fundierte naturwissenschaftliche Kenntnisse. Dies geht aus seinem brillanten Aufsatz 'On the Formation and Various Properties of Musical Sound' hervor, das den Auftakt des Buches bildet.

Der vollständige Titel des Werkes lautet:
The Art of Playing / The German Flute / on new principles / calculated to increase its powers and give to it / greater variety, expression and effect / to which are added / copious examples in an elegant stile, a compleat / system of Modulation, the art of varying / simple passages and a new method of tonguing. / By / John Gunn / teacher of the German Flute & Violoncello / 'Est quoddam prodire tenus, si non datur ultra.' Hor. / Sold by the Author etc.

Aufgrund von Kritiken in 'The Critical Review' vom Oktober 1793 sowie in 'The Monthly Review' vom Dezember 1793 kann das Jahr 1793 als Erscheinungsjahr gelten.[3] Neuauflagen erschienen in den Jahren 1795 und 1807; sie deuten auf eine erfolgreiche Verbreitung des Buches hin.

Welche Bedeutung hat 'The Art of Playing' seinerzeit gehabt und welches Interesse sollte heute noch dieser Flötenschule entgegengebracht werden? Zunächst einmal zählt das Werk durch seinen Stil und die Art der Themenbehandlung zu den interessantesten historischen Flötenschulen überhaupt. Dabei ist allerdings einschränkend zu sagen, dass Authentizitätsfanatiker von heute, die nur nach konkreten Vorschriften fahnden, möglicherweise schlecht bedient sind: der Text liefert nicht so viele Hinweise in bezug auf Artikulation oder Ornamentik, wie es in anderen, vor allem älteren Instrumentalschulen üblich war. Stattdessen werden die einzelnen Aspekte in einer seltenen Kombination von wissenschaftlicher Objektivität und künstlerisch-persönlicher Stellungnahme abgehandelt. Die Schule ist sowohl für die einklappige, als auch für die mehrklappige Flöte (bis zu 6 Klappen) geeignet.

International betrachtet gebührt dem Werk ein gleichrangiger Platz neben den heute viel bekannteren Flötenschulen von Tromlitz (1791) und Devienne (ca. 1792), von denen Gunn übrigens aller Wahrscheinlichkeit nach nichts gewusst haben dürfte. In der Entwicklung der englischen Methoden der zweiten Jahrhunderthälfte aber ragt die Arbeit von Gunn weit heraus: die wichtigsten seiner Vorgänger wie Granom, Heron, Arnold und Wragg[4] wendeten sich in erster Linie an ein Amateurpublikum, wobei es darauf ankam, so schnell wie möglich und 'without assistance of a Master' zu Elementarfähigkeiten zu gelangen.

Die einzige Schule, in der ein professioneller Ton herrscht, ist die englische Übersetzung von Quantz' 1752 publiziertem 'Versuch ...', welche unter dem Titel 'Easy and Fundamental Instructions' erst 1780 bei Welcker in London erschienen war.

Dass Gunn Quantz' Versuch wohl gekannt hat, geht daraus hervor, dass er dessen Adagio als Beispiel für das freie Auszieren einer Melodie, von Gunn 'Variation' oder 'Embellishment' genannt, im Text zitiert und im Notenanhang vollständig abgedruckt hat. Ausserdem sind sämtliche Tabellen zur Verzierung einzelner Intervalle aus Quantz' Versuch übernommen, was darauf schliessen lässt, dass die Praxis der 'freien' (Quantz sagt 'willkürlichen') Verzierung in England noch weit verbreitet war. Auch Gunn's ausführliche Unterweisung in der 'Kunst des Modulierens', erst sinnvoll geworden durch die zusätzlichen Klappen, welche das Spielen in erweiterten Tonarten ermöglichten, weist in diese Richtung: das Material stellt eine Art praktische Harmonielehre zum Improvisieren in fast allen Tonarten dar. Gleichzeitig bilden sie 'Exercises' im Sinne der späteren Etüde, die bereits progressiv geordnet sind. Gunn's Verzierungs- und Modulationslehre legt Zeugnis davon ab, dass auch um die Wende zum 19. Jahrhundert das Komponieren und Interpretieren von Musik noch eng miteinander verknüpft waren.

Wenn auch in 'The Art of Playing' der Einfluss von Quantz nachweisbar ist, so geht Gunn im

Bereich der Ornamentik neue Wege. Selbst fasst er dies folgendermassen zusammen:
'The modern refinements in the performance of music ... have certainly not increased the
number of what are strictly called *graces*, but, on the contrary, have considerably diminished
their number and greatly simplified them. The performers of the old school had much of what
may be called the *graces of the finger* than the modern, which cultivates more the expression of
the *bow* and the management of *tone*.'

Zum einen werden hier in einem Atem Streicher- und Flötentechnik genannt; die Tendenz,
Bogentechnik auf der Flöte zu imitieren, sollte sich im 19. Jahrhundert weiter durchsetzen.
Zum anderen hatte eine Veränderung stattgefunden, nicht nur bei der Verzierung, diesem
Eckpfeiler der 'alten' Schule, sondern auch bei der Artikulation. Ist bei Tromlitz (1791) die
'wahre Sprache auf diesem Instrument' noch eine der Schwerpunkte der Flötentechnik
überhaupt,[5] bei Gunn ist sie auf wenige Essentialia zusammengeschrumpft: auf einen freien
Gebrauch des Zungenstosses und eine grosszügige Anwendung von Bindebögen.[6] Stossen und
Binden sind gleichbedeutend geworden und nicht länger gekoppelt an eine 'idiomgebundene'
Aussprache einer musikalischen Figur.[7]

Was ist also noch übrig von der 'alten' Vortragslehre? Gunn behandelt lediglich die wichtigsten
Verzierungen, wie Triller,[8] Doppelschlag, Fingervibrato[9] und, natürlich, den Vorschlag,[10] der
noch immer prinzipiell lang ist und auf den Schlag kommt. Er soll immer mit einem 'messa di
voce' (< >) versehen sein. Ausserdem soll die Auflösung immer kurz gespielt werden, wie
beim sogenannten 'Abzug'.[11]

Bei Gunn findet sich eine in älteren Flötenschulen öfter anzutreffende Spielweise von
Synkopen, wobei die zweite Hälfte der synkopierenden Note, welche auf den 'guten' Taktteil
kommt, leicht mit dem Atem artikuliert werden soll: ♪ ♩ ♪ wird ♪♪♪♪ ausgeführt. Delusse
(1761), Heron (1771) und Tromlitz (1791) geben ähnliche Anweisungen,[11] die möglicherweise
darauf hinweisen, daß auch am Ende des 18. Jahrhunderts die alten Prinzipien zur richtigen
Aussprache der 'guten' und 'schlechten' Taktteile weiterhin angewandt wurden.

Viel ausführlicher behandelt Gunn die neuen, 'modernen' Themen wie die Technik der
Doppelzunge und die Tonbildung in all ihren Aspekten: Tonqualität, Klangfarbe, Intonation
und Dynamik und - nicht zuletzt - die wechselseitigen Zusammenhänge dieser Teilaspekte.

Was die Doppelzunge betrifft, so unterscheidet Gunn zwei Arten: die übliche Methode, bei der
die zweite Silbe immer die schwächere ist ('the second is articulated ... in a less distinct manner,
by the reaction of the tongue ... by pronouncing the syllables *diddle*') und eine neue, von ihm
selbst erfundene Methode, wobei die jetzt als Nachteil empfundene, ungleiche Qualität beider
Silben aufgehoben sein soll: 'The two syllables that are by one action and reaction to articulate
two notes, are *teddy* or *tiddy*, which, when pronounced for some time very distinctly and
afterwards softening the consonants as much as possible, will acquire a volubility as great as the
other double tongue, but infinitely more articulate and distinct.'[12]

Es ist klar, dass die qualitative Gleichheit der Artikulationssilben eine ganz 'moderne'
Forderung darstellte; sie wurde erst viel später, etwa in der Schule von Drouet (um 1830)
allgemein praktiziert.[13] In den englischen Schulen aber herrschen auch dann noch
Kombinationen wie 'tootle' oder 'diddle' vor.[14]

Der Tonbildung widmet Gunn mehrere Kapitel. Schon im Abschnitt 'On the Formation ... of

Musical Sound' werden die Zusammenhänge zwischen Atemdruck und Atemmenge sowie ihr Einfluss auf Tonhöhe bzw. Stärke des Tons untersucht - mit einer exemplarischen Klarheit, die man oft sogar in heutigen Flötenschulen vergeblich sucht. Darüberhinaus stellt Gunn fest, dass in Analogie zur Tonbildung bei Sängern, die mit Hilfe eines einzigen winzigen Organs, der Glottis,[15] eine unendliche Zahl von Tonhöhen, Klangfarben und -stärken produzieren können, auch das Embouchure bei der Flöte ähnliches vermag:

'Astonishing, indeed, is this power of contracting and dilating the muscles or ligaments, by which this aperture is said to be so minutely and almost infinitely varied ... It would be impossible to produce that beautifull effect, called a swell or *messa di voce*, ... if this power of increasing the velocity of air cannot be done in a considerable degree without any additional compression of the aperture ... The different degrees of velocity of the air, therefore, by whatever means produced, are the uniform and only causes of gravity and acuteness; ... the loudness of sounds will be always in direct proportion to the quantity ... of the column of air employed.'

Interessant sind hier auch die Hinweise auf die Parallelität von Musik und Malerei. Gunn vergleicht - und das kommt immer wieder im Verlauf des Textes zurück - die Elemente beider Disziplinen: Tonhöhe - Kontur, dynamische Schattierung - Perspektive, Timbre - Farbe, Resonanz - Lichtreflexion usw.

Über die Rolle der Resonanz ist Gunn sehr ausführlich: er erklärt die Funktion der harmonischen Teiltöne und ihre Wirkung im Zusammenhang mit der Beschaffenheit des Klangkörpers. Im Kapitel 'Of Tone, or the Embouchure' vermittelt er ausserdem einen Einblick in zusätzliche Faktoren der Tonbildung: Blasrichtung, Haltung des Instruments und des Kopfes sowie die Technik des Überblasens. Eine seiner Beobachtungen besteht darin, dass bei bestimmten optimalen Verhältnissen sich harmonische Teiltöne beim Anblasen gegenseitig und echoartig verstärken - ein theoretischer Tatbestand, der auch im praktischen Bereich wichtige Konsequenzen hat.

Gunn zeigt damit eine, für damals wie heute seltene Kombinationsgabe von wissenschaftlichen und praktischen Erkenntnissen, die erst später, etwa mit der Person von Theobald Boehm, deutlicher in Erscheinung tritt. Aber gleichzeitig ist es interessant darauf hinzuweisen, dass im Bereich des Flötenbaus und der Flötenakustik nicht erst bei Boehm 'empirisch' gewonnene Erkenntnisse durch 'wissenschaftliche' Planung verdrängt werden. Zweifellos gehört auch Gunn zu denen, die einem Genie wie Theobald Boehm den Weg geebnet haben. Ein letztes Beispiel von Gunn's akustischer Beobachtungsgabe:

'There is a loudness or intensity of sound, which depends solely on the *density* or compression of the air and is always in proportion to it, which accounts for the different effects of sounds in different states of the atmosphere; and consequently the compressed tone of a flute that is not smothered, must be louder, *caeteris paribus*, than that which is not compressed, but loudness, from this cause, has a sort of *hardness* in it, whilst that caused by an increase of volume, and less compressed, is more soft and mellow.'

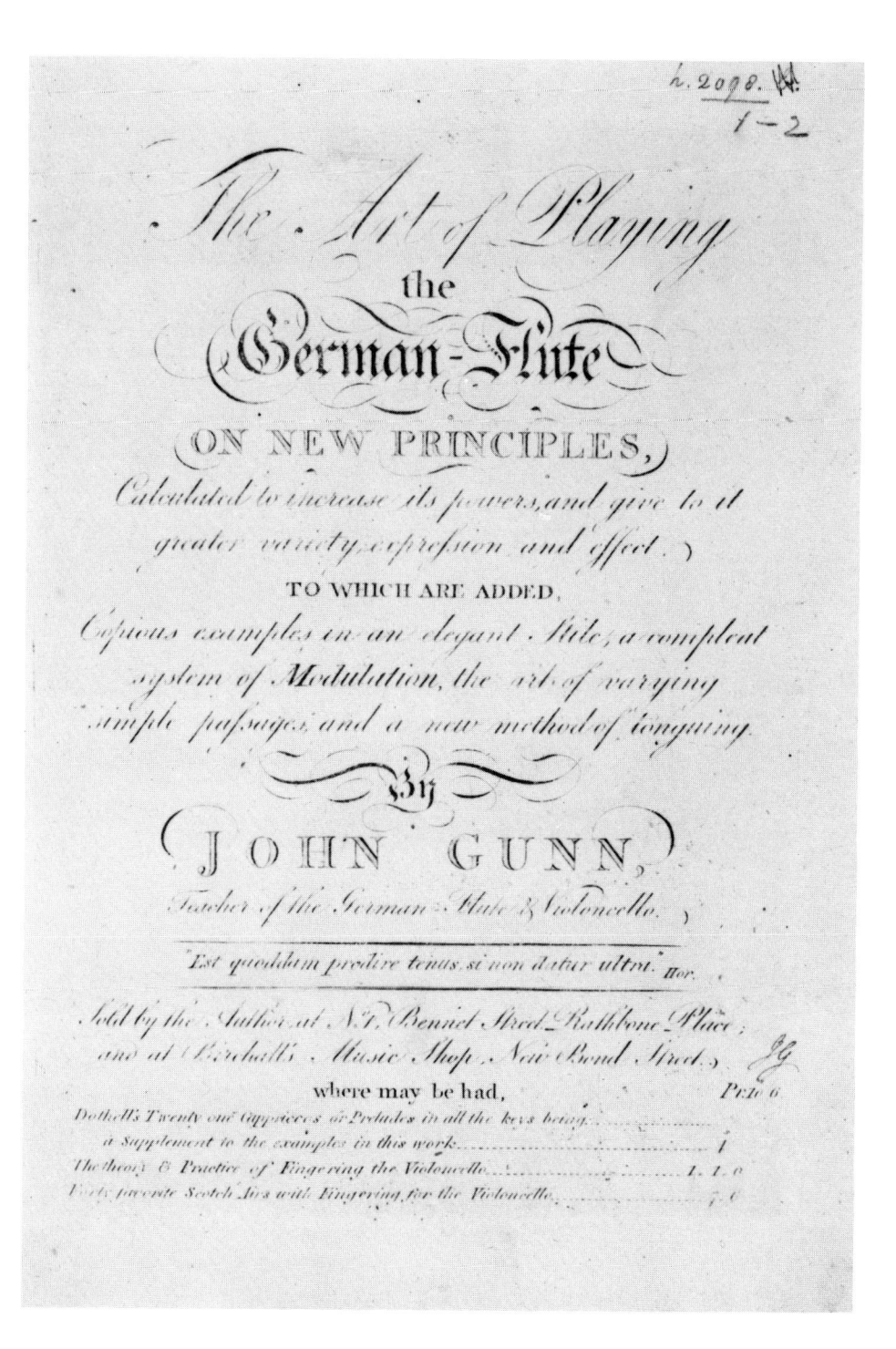

John Gunn, *The Art of Playing the German Flute on New Principles* (1793), Titelseite.

Aus John Gunn, *The Art of Playing the German Flute on New Principles* (1793).

Eine weitere Besonderheit in der Flötenschule Gunn's ist die Aufmerksamkeit, die er dem Thema der musikalischen Expressivität widmet. Sowohl in Kap. VII 'Of the Method and proper Objects of Practice' als in dem speziell dem Thema gewidmeten Kapitel 'Of musical Expression' stossen wir auf interessante Bemerkungen:

'The principles of Musical Expression have never been properly investigated, nor have their agreement or disagreement with the principles of oratorical expression or elocution, as far as I know, been ever clearly pointed out.' (S. 24)

Ausserdem ist er der Meinung, dass 'every variety and modification of sound, that words or periods can receive, the mere articulation of the former alone excepted, are to be considered as properties of musical sounds. Taking, therefore, oratorical expression with me as a guide ...'

Zu den primären Erfordernissen für einen expressiven Vortrag zählt Gunn das richtige Akzentuieren. In 'Of Musical Expression' heisst es:

'The most simple and obvious distinction between a succession of musical sounds in respect to expression, is that of their being 'accented' or 'unaccented'.' (S. 24)

Dabei unterscheidet er zwischen qualitativem Akzent (Agogik) und dynamischem Akzent ('Emphasis'). Er gibt Beispiele für beide Formen, wobei er auch darauf hinweist, welche wichtige Rolle die alten Versformen wie Jambe oder Dactylus bei der Gestaltung des musikalischen Rhythmus spielen. So erklärt er, dass die Versfüsse Spondee und Dactylus sich mehr für gerade Takte eignen, die Molossus-, Jambe- und Trochäusformen aber mehr für ungerade Taktarten.

Darüberhinaus vermittelt er einen Einblick in die Kunst des Phrasierens, wobei er nicht nur auf Satzbau und Periodisierung, sondern auch auf die Funktion der harmonischen Struktur hinweist. Zur Demonstration der dargelegten Prinzipien verwendet er Ausdrücke wie 'antecedent' und 'consequent' sowie kleine Symbole zur Markierung der einzelnen Phrasen und Teilphrasen. Dies alles, zusammen mit seinen Ausführungen in bezug auf die Länge der Phrasen sowie auf den Begriff der Symmetrie, ist bereits als ein erster Schritt zur Etablierung einer Formenanalyse zu werten.

Als weitere Themen bei der Kunst des musikalischen Ausdrucks behandelt Gunn die Forderung nach Abwechslung ('variety'), die, wie er sagt, 'in unserer menschlichen Natur' begründet ist. Das Spiel mit Licht und Schatten ('Chiaro-scuro'), zu dem in erster Linie alle dynamischen Schattierungen gehören, zählt er zu den wichtigsten Merkmalen der musikalischen Gestaltung, da in seiner Sicht die dynamische Differenzierung gleichzusetzen ist mit den verschiedenen Stufen von Betonung in der Sprache. Da aber die Musik - und durch sie 'the emotions of the soul' - von allen Völkern und allen Individuen verstanden werden kann, hat sie als Kommunikationssystem einen universalen Anspruch, der in mancher Hinsicht über den der Sprache hinausragt:

'... everyone knows that it is not merely the words made use of itself that ... engages our confidence or affection ... but that all these opposite and different shades of meaning are conveyed to us by the *tone, emphasis* and *expression of the sound* with which it is uttered. Every emotion, affection and passion of the soul, therefore, having its peculiar inflexion of voice and appropriated expression and quality of sound...' (S. 27)

Aus alledem ergibt sich - so Gunn - für den Flötisten die Notwendigkeit, sein Instrument sowohl im *Forte* als auch im *Piano* besser als bisher zu beherrschen. Ausserdem, so betont Gunn immer wieder, gehören nicht nur technische Aspekte zur richtigen Aufführung, sondern auch die Bildung des musikalischen Geschmacks:

'... Indeed, the prevailing want of expression and pathos, in this and other instruments, may be ascribed not so much to the want of feeling and abilities in learners, as to a defience of the known rules of art ...'[16]

'... Experience has shown, that it is more easy to acquire a facility in making embellishments, than a correct taste to direct their application ...'[17]

Zum Schluss noch eine Bemerkung über den methodischen Aufbau des Buches. Obwohl der Text (32 Seiten) und die musikalischen Beispiele (53 Seiten) ähnlich wie z.B. bei Quantz voneinander getrennt sind, lassen sich doch erste Andeutungen für einen progressiven Aufbau erkennen. Sowohl in bezug auf die Reihenfolge als auch auf den Inhalt der Kapitel ist das Material schrittweise geordnet. Ausserdem sind Übungen zur Überwindung sowohl technischer als musikalischer Probleme vorhanden. In dieser Hinsicht stand Gunn damals zweifellos in der vordersten Reihe einer neuen Entwicklung, wobei im Vermitteln von Sachkenntnissen auch der Lernende erstmals 'methodisch' miteinbezogen wird.

Zusammenfassend kann man feststellen, dass 'The Art of Playing the German Flute' nicht nur ein überaus interessantes Dokument des klassischen Flötenspiels ist, sondern darüberhinaus einen Einblick in vielerlei Aspekte des musikalischen Denkens der damaligen Zeit gibt. Seine Schule hat noch Jahrzehnte später bei prominenten Flötisten Beachtung gefunden: um 1828/30 hat Th. Lindsay in seinem Buch 'Elements of Flute Playing' Gunn's Aufsatz 'On the Formation ... of Musical Sound' vollständig abgedruckt. Mit vollem Recht konnte Gunn den Anspruch erheben, seine 'Kunst des Flötenspiels'[18] auf neue Prinzipien gegründet zu haben. Denn wenige seiner Zeitgenossen haben so klar - praktisch, aber auch theoretisch - erkannt, dass das Spiel auf der Flöte, die sich ohnehin nur schwer neben den anderen Holzblasinstrumenten behaupten konnte, an die neuen Forderungen des Musiklebens angepasst werden musste. Sämtliche strukturbestimmenden Faktoren wie Form, Dynamik und Artikulation, aber auch Instrumentenbau, Grösse der Ensembles und des Klangbereichs erweiterten sich ja sehr schnell. Gunn hat versucht, in einer für Professionelle, aber auch für Laien verständlichen Sprache, die Flötentechnik in das neue musikalische Gesamtgefüge einzuordnen. Dabei hat er als erster konsequent wissenschaftliche, vor allem akustische Erkenntnisse mitberücksichtigt. Auch im schwer zu konkretisierenden, ja heiklen Bereich des musikalischen Ausdrucks zeigt er eine scharfe Beobachtungsgabe. Aber man kann feststellen, dass Gunn, obwohl er sich auf natur - wie auf geisteswissenschaftlicher Ebene gleichermassen weit vorgewagt hat, dies nicht um des Selbstzwecks willen tat, sondern um zu höheren künstlerischen Leistungen zu gelangen, bzw. um anderen dazu zu verhelfen.

Gunn kannte auch die Grenzen eines solchen Unterfangens. Man kann das vielleicht aus dem lateinischen Satzmotiv ableiten, das er auf die Titelseite seines Werkes geschrieben hat: 'Est quoddam prodire tenus, si non datur ultra.'[19]

Anmerkungen

1 Die zweite Flötenschule erschien 1794 mit dem Titel
'The School of the German Flute, or Principles & Practice.'

2 Überliefert sind nur 'Forty Scotch Airs for Flute, Violin and Cello.'

3 Nach Th. E. Warner: Indication of Performance Practice in Woodwind Instruction Books, New York 1964, S. 334.

4 L. Granom: Plain and Easy Instructions for Playing on the German Flute, London 1766.
L. Heron: A Treatise on the German Flute, London 1771.
S. Arnold: Dr. Arnolds New Instructions for the German Flute, London 1787.
J. Wragg: The Flute Perceptor, London ca. 1792.

5 Tromlitz widmet den verschiedenen Artikulationsmustern mehr als 80 Seiten (Ausführlicher und gründlicher Unterricht die Flöte zu spielen, Kap. VIII und IX).

6 Noch 1771 heisst es in Heron's Treatise: 'I would by no means have you falling into a custom of slurring ...' (S. 34).

7 Devienne verwendet sogar eine einzige Figur zur Demonstration vielfältiger Kombinationen von Binden und Stossen und belegt damit ihre Austauschbarkeit.

8 Kap. VI, S. 18

9 Flattement, von Gunn als 'Sweetening' übersetzt, übrigens die einzige von ihm erwähnte Vibratoart.

10 Immer von der oberen Nebennote ausgehend.

11 Delusse, L'Art..., S. 4 und planche 10, gibt die Artikulation T, hé für Synkopen. Heron, Treatise S. 33, schreibt: '... the second receiving an emphasis with the breath.' Tromlitz, Unterricht S. 182, gibt tää für synkopierende Noten.

12 Kap. IV, 'Of Tonguing', S. 14.

13 'dou-gue' oder 'de-re'.

14 Th. Lindsay: Elements of Flute Playing, London 1828/30, S. 105.

15 In Kombination mit variablen Atemdruck- und Atemmengeverhältnissen.

16 Introduction, S. 1.

17 Kap. X 'Of Variatons or Embellishments', S. 32.

18 Ein Titel, den man sonst kaum bei Flötenschulen antrifft.

19 Nach Horaz: 'Man kann nur bis zu einem gewissen Punkt gelangen, wenn es einem nicht gegeben ist weiterzukommen.'

Friedrich Ludwig Dulon

F.L. Dulon, der blinde Flötenspieler (1769-1826)
Über 'Leben und Meynungen' eines reisenden Virtuosen

Karl Ventzke

1 Stationen seines Lebens

Friedrich Ludwig Dulon (Dülon), Flötenvirtuose und 'Bearbeiter' einer bis zum Jahre 1787 berichtenden Beschreibung seines eigenen Lebens,[1] wurde nach seiner Angabe am 14. August 1769 in Oranienburg an der Havel geboren. Sein Vater Louis Dulon (1741-um 1798), gelernter Goldschmied und zu jener Zeit Steuer-Inspektor in Oranienburg, hatte in Potsdam Flötenunterricht bei Augustin Neuff (Neif), einem Schüler von J. J. Quantz, erhalten. Sechs Wochen nach seiner Geburt erblindete der junge Dulon infolge ärztlicher Fehlbehandlung bis auf einen geringen Lichtschimmer.

Seine Eltern verzogen um 1774 nach Havelberg und von dort 1777 nach Stendal, wo der Achtjährige Privatunterricht in der französischen Sprache bekam. 1778 wurde Dulon durch einen in Stendal auftretenden blinden Flötisten namens Josef Winter zu eigenem Flötenspiel angeregt. Sein Vater unterrichtete ihn darin durch häufiges Vorlesen aus Quantz' 'Versuch einer Anweisung die Floete traversiere zu spielen'. Bald komponierte der junge Dulon sogar selber. Im Kontrapunkt und Klavierspiel unterwies ihn Johann Karl Angerstein, damals Organist und Lehrer in Stendal, später Pfarrer in Bertkow bei Stendal.

Ein phänomenales Gedächtnis[2] und außergewöhnliche Begabung erlaubten Dulon, erstmals 1779 in Stendal öffentlich aufzutreten und, 12 Jahre alt, von September bis November 1781 seine erste Kunstreise auszuführen. Sein Vater, der deswegen später seine Position als Steuer-Inspektor aufgab, oder auch seine ganze Familie begleiteten ihn in den frühen Jahren auf diesen Kunstreisen, über deren Stationen jetzt ein Überblick gegeben werden soll.

Dulons erste 'musikalische Wanderung' führte den Zwölfjährigen zunächst nach Potsdam, wo er den Flötenlehrer seines Vaters kennenlernte, und dann nach Berlin, wo er Johann Philipp Kirnberger (1721-1783) begegnete. Mitte 1782 folgte eine kurze Reise nach Magdeburg. Die nächste Kunstreise begann im November 1782 und hatte wieder Berlin zum Ziel; Dulon lernte Johann Friedrich Reichardt (1752-1814) sowie den Kronprinzen Friedrich Wilhelm (1744-1797) kennen und kehrte im Dezember über Potsdam und Brandenburg nach Stendal zurück. - Die vierte musikalische Wanderung Dulons begann bereits im Januar 1783 und dauerte bis Mitte März. Folgende Städte wurden dabei besucht: Ludwigslust, Hamburg (hier Bekanntschaft mit Carl Philipp Emanuel Bach), Altona, Lüneburg, Lüchow (Besuch bei Dr. med. J.J.H. Ribock[3]) und Salzwedel.

Im Juli 1783 brachen Vater und Sohn Dulon zu einer größeren Kunstreise auf. In Potsdam nahm der Junior Unterricht bei Karl Benda (1748-1836), dort lernte er auch Franz Benda (1709-1786) und dessen Neffen Friedrich (1746-1793) kennen und gab am 12. August 1783 ein öffentliches Konzert. Die weiteren Stationen der langen Reise waren: Oranienburg, Reinsberg,

Neubrandenburg, Prenzlau, Schwedt/Oder, Stettin, Stargard, Anklam, Greifswald, Stralsund, Rostock (1.12.83), Lübeck, Eutin (1.1.84), Hamburg, Stade, Bremen, Oldenburg (9.4.84), Hannover, Celle, wieder Hannover, Braunschweig, Wolfenbüttel, nochmals Hannover (7.7.84), Helmstedt (25.8.84), Halberstadt (Begegnung mit dem Dichter Johann Gleim), Quedlinburg, Magdeburg (17.9.84), Zerbst, Dessau, Halle, Köthen (1.11.84), Leipzig (9.11.84), dann wieder Dessau und schließlich Magdeburg, wo die ganze Familie endlich wieder zusammenkam. In Halle machte Dulon Bekanntschaft mit Johann Adam Hiller (1728-1804) und Daniel Gottlob Türk (1750-1813); in Leipzig suchte er den Flötisten Johann George Tromlitz (1725-1805) auf.[4]

Von Magdeburg aus nahm eine nunmehr jahrelange, ununterbrochene Wanderschaft der Familie Dulon ihren Anfang. Wir können sie nur bis zum Jahre 1787 verfolgen, ohne zu wissen, wann und wo sie eigentlich zu Ende war.

Über Quedlinburg, Blankenburg (3.1.85), Halberstadt und Helmstedt begaben sich die Dulons nach Hannover, wo man sich mit Dr. Ribock traf. In Göttingen lernten sie den gelehrten Dr. Johann Nikolaus Forkel (1749-1818) kennen. Auf dem Wege nach Mainz (Ankunft 28.3.85) kam man durch die Städte Kassel, Marburg und Frankfurt am Main.

Von Mainz aus reisten Vater und Sohn Dulon in die Schweiz: sie kamen durch Worms, Straßburg, Kolmar, Mühlhausen, Basel (2.5.85), Olten, Aarau, Solothurn und kehrten zurück über Straßburg, Karlsruhe, Mannheim und Worms.

Nach kurzem Erholungsaufenthalt in Mainz ging die Reise im Juli 1785 weiter über Koblenz, Bad Ems, Bonn und Aachen nach Spa in der Provinz Lüttich, von dort über Aachen zurück nach Köln, Düsseldorf, Wesel, Kleve (9.9.85), Nimwegen, Emmerich, Xanten (20.10.85), Krefeld, Düsseldorf, Elberfeld und dann über Düsseldorf und Wesel wieder nach Kleve, wo die Familie Aufenthalt nahm. Vater und Sohn Dulon besuchten alsdann die niederländischen Städte Arnheim, Zutphen, Utrecht, Amsterdam (13.1.86), Leiden (1.2.86), Haarlem und Rotterdam; hier konzertierte Dulon mit Abt Vogler (1749-1814).

Am 11. März 1786 verließen die beiden Dulons die Niederlande auf dem Seewege und landeten am 13.3. abends bei Harwich, von wo aus die Reise nach London weiterging. Dulon trat in London öffentlich auf und hatte Kontakt mit den berühmtesten Musikerpersönlichkeiten jener Zeit. Im Juni 1786 verließ man das britische Inselreich via Dover. - Während der Weiterreise auf dem Festland kam die Reisegesellschaft durch Calais, Dunkirchen, Brügge, Gent, Brüssel (12.7.86), Mecheln, Antwerpen, Löwen, Lüttich, Maastricht; über Aachen wurde Köln am 30.8.1786 erreicht.

Die letzten bekannten Stationen dieser Reise waren Düsseldorf, Dorsten, Münster (22.9.86), Osnabrück, Hannover (14.10.86), Einbeck, Göttingen (bis 12.12.86 mit formeller Aufnahme Dulons in die reformierte Kirche), Alfeld, Hildesheim (29.12.86), nochmals Hannover, Minden (16.1.87) und Bückeburg. Für 1787 plante man, das Frühjahr in Westfalen, den Sommer in den Rheingegenden und den folgenden Winter in der Schweiz zu verbringen.

Im Text der Lebensbeschreibung Dulons werden beiläufig noch folgende Aufenthalte der späteren Jahre erwähnt: Tübingen 1789, Berlin und Wien 1791, Lübeck 1795, Minden 1796, Köthen, Glatz und Breslau 1798. Aus anderen Quellen sind als Reisestationen noch bekannt: Hamburg 1796, Meiningen, Leipzig und Berlin 1798.

Konnten wir die bis jetzt genannten und sehr genauen Daten seines Lebenslaufes Dulons eigener veröffentlichter Beschreibung entnehmen, so sind wir für Angaben über seinen weiteren Lebensweg auf zeitgenössische Quellen und Berichte anderer angewiesen.

Gerber berichtet, daß Dulon seit 1796 'russisch-kaiserlicher Kammermusiker zu Petersburg' gewesen sei, 1798 aber wieder sein Vaterland besuchte; 'Gegenwärtig (1800) hat er sich zu Stendal in der Altmark angekauft, macht von da aus, die Winter über, kleine Reisen, und bringt die Sommer im Genusse der Kunst und des Wohlstandes, den seine Pension aus Rußland befördert, auf seinem Landgute zu'.[5]

Nach Schilling wurde Dulon 1792 vom 'damaligen Großfürsten von Rußland mit 1000 Rubel jährlichem Gehalt' engagiert und kam 1795 nach Petersburg; 'nach der Zeit kaufte er sich bei Waldenburg ein kleines Landgut, um hier seine noch übrige Lebenszeit in Ruhe zuzubringen'[6] - ein wahrlich schöner Aspekt für einen Dreißigjährigen!

Daß Dulon nahe Stendal wieder ansässig wurde, mag mit seinem jüngeren Bruder Friedrich Wilhelm (1772-1849) zu tun gehabt haben, der seit 1796 Postkommissar, später Postdirektor in Stendal war.[7]
Offensichtlich hatte Dulon, 'ein besserer Wirth als die meisten seiner Kollegen', im Oktober 1799 die Absicht, 'von dem Ertrag seiner Reisen ein artiges Landgut in Chursachsen, in der schönen Gegend von Waldenburg' zu kaufen.[8] Dieser Plan wurde aber nicht realisiert; im September 1800 wußte die A.M.Z. zu melden, daß sich 'der rühmlich bekannte . . . Dulon zu Stendal in der Altmark angekauft' habe.[9]

Konzertbesprechungen in der A.M.Z. geben Hinweise auf folgende weitere Stationen:
Leipzig - April 1799, Juni 1800, Januar 1804, Januar 1806, Februar 1809 und November 1810;
Berlin - März 1803 und Februar 1804;
Frankfurt/Main - Januar 1805;
Hannover - Juni 1808;
Meiningen - August 1811.
Aus dem später noch zu behandelnden Briefwechsel Wieland/Dulon ist zu entnehmen, daß sich Dulon 1806 in Dresden und 1807 in Kiel und in Dänemark aufhielt. Im 'Journal des Luxus und der Moden'[10] wird ausführlich über Konzerte berichtet, die Dulon in Weimar im September 1805, Dezember 1808 und Januar 1809 gab; in Halle trat er im März 1806 auf.

Am 31. Mai 1813 bezog Dulon Wohnung in Würzburg.[11] Was ihn veranlaßte, hier seßhaft zu werden, ist näher nicht bekannt, dürfte aber mit der ihn betreuenden Familie Reinstein zu erklären sein.

Als 'lediger Musicus' verstarb Dulon in Würzburg am Nachmittag des 7. Juli 1826 an Zehrfieber.[12] Ein längerer Nachruf erschien im 'Neuen Nekrolog der Deutschen', 4. Jahrgang 1826, Ilmenau 1828.
Aus seiner Würzburger Zeit sind besondere Nachrichten offenbar nicht mehr überliefert. Im Jahre 1824 veröffentliche Dulon, dessen Fertigkeit Sinngedichte zu verfassen, schon Gerber hervorhob, noch folgendes

*'Epigramm
auf alle gute, vortreffliche und schlechte
Tonsetzer, Schriftsteller und Sprecher gemünzt:*

*Wer Viel mit Vielem sagen kann,
ist immer ein verdienter Mann.*

*Doch Viel mit Wenigem zu sagen
gilt mehr!
Wer's kann, sey hochgeehrt;
er ist der Klugen Beifall werth,
ist werth, dass alle nach ihm fragen.*

*Doch nimmer wird nach dem gefragt,
der uns mit Vielem Wenig sagt!*

Dulon, der blinde Flötenspieler.' [13]

Als 'Dulon der blinde Flötenspieler' war er aufgrund einer näher nicht bestimmbaren Mischung von anerkannter künstlerischer Leistung und 'mitleidiger Rücksicht auf sein Schicksal' zu Lebzeiten berühmt geworden; er ging auch so in die Nachwelt ein.

Sein Leben als blinder Mensch blieb verbunden mit dem Mit-Leben und der ständigen Begleitung mindestens eines anderen, sehenden Menschen. Wer begleitete ihn, wer sah und arbeitete erforderlichenfalls für ihn, wer ermöglichte Dulons weitere Tätigkeit, als seine Angehörigen, insbesondere sein um 1798 verstorbener Vader,[14] diese Pflicht nicht mehr erfüllen konnten?

'Mein guter Genius in weiblicher Gestalt' - so nannte Dulon jene Frau, die am 15. Januar 1786 in Amsterdam seine ständige Begleiterin wurde. Und er gab ihr, 'obschon sie nicht mit mir unter einem Herzen gelegen, . . . öffentlich den Namen . . . einer Schwester'. Er bezeichnete sie als 'die Reinstein' und erläuterte dazu, daß sie ihn bereits fünf Jahre begleitet hatte, 'als sie dem Besitzer dieses Namens ihre Hand gab'.[15] - Sie beherrschte die französische Sprache gut und besorgte bald nach ihrem Kennenlernen Dulons Geldgeschäfte.[16]

'Ohne sie wäre ich mein ganzes Leben hindurch geblieben, was ich zuvor war; das heißt ein rohes, unkultiviertes und außerhalb dem Gebiete der Musik für jede menschliche Gesellschaft unbrauchbares Subject; ... so ist sie nunmehr siebenzehn Jahre hindurch die Gefährtin meiner Tage, und wird es hoffentlich bleiben' - soweit Dulon im Jahre 1803 über diese Frau.[17] Sie war offenbar verehelicht mit dem Musiker Martin Joseph Reinstein aus Würzburg, über den es 1808 in den 'Artistisch-literarischen Blättern von und für Franken' heißt: '... Martin (Reinstein) ist ein fertiger Spieler auf der Violin und ein seines Lehrers, des berühmten Violinisten Baimel zu Bamberg, würdiger Schüler. Er befindet sich seit längerer Zeit her und noch gegenwärtig mit dem erblindeten Dulon, dem weltbekannten Flötenspieler, dessen Schwager er ist, auf Reisen'. Martin Reinstein war - wie zwei seiner Brüder - später Mitglied der großherzoglichen Kapelle in Würzburg.[18] - Näheres über 'die Reinstein' müßte noch erforscht werden.

Als Komponist ist Dulon mit fünf Werken an die Öffentlichkeit getreten, die zwischen 1800 und 1810 bei Breitkopf & Härtel in Leipzig erschienen; es sind Kompositionen mit und für Flöte.[19]

Das hier beigegebene Bildnis Dulons aus der Zeit um 1800 hat einen in der Sammlung des Verfassers aufbewahrten Kupferstich von Johann Gottfried Scheffner (1765-1825) nach einer Miniatur von August Ritt (1765-1799) zur Vorlage.[20]

2 Zum Inhalt der Selbstbiographie Dulons

Der anonym arbeitende Rezensent der A.M.Z., vermutlich ihr Redakteur Johann Friedrich Rochlitz (1769-1842), - 'er kennet D. persönlich und hat, wenn auch keinen Scheffel Salz, doch manchen interessanten Abend mit ihm genossen' - war mit dem Inhalt der Arbeit nicht so recht zufrieden: die von ihm erwarteten neuen Offenbarungen eines blinden Künstlers wurden 'gar nicht gegeben'; der 'verehrungswürdige Vater Wieland' hatte das nach Meinung des Rezensenten 'erwünschte Arrondieren und Annullieren, wie es scheint, nirgens ausüben wollen'; schließlich aber forderte er, Dulon möge sich seine Leser als vermeintliche gute Bekannte 'bedeutender, unterrichteter, ernster, weniger müßig und auch etwas vornehmer' vorstellen - und für solche schreiben![21]

Es mag sein, daß der literarische Wert dieser Lebenserinnerungen trotz der Veredelungsarbeit des großen Weimarer Dichters Christoph Martin Wieland (1733-1813) weithin im Durchschnittlichen blieb. Höher ist jedoch für jeden Beurteiler der musikgeschichtliche Wert zu veranschlagen. War es schon zu Wielands Zeiten 'das einzige Buch seiner Art', so ist das Angebot in dieser 'Art' - in Biographien von Flötisten oder Holzbläsern überhaupt - inzwischen kaum besser geworden.

Auch in unserer Zeit mag es nicht jedermanns Art sein, in der von dem A.M.Z.-Rezensenten beanstandeten 'Weitläufigkeit und Redseligkeit' des Plaudertones unterhalten und informiert zu werden; indessen urteilte Schilling, daß die 'sehr anziehende Lebensbeschreibung ... namentlich von jungen Künstlern oft und mit Aufmerksamkeit gelesen werden sollte, da sie ungemein viel Lehrreiches für sie enthält.'[22]

Dulon stand bei Zeitgenossen im Ruf, 'einer der ersten Flöttraversisten von Europa'[23] zu sein. Sein Flötenspiel wurde teilweise überschwenglich gefeiert. Durch seine ausgedehnte Reisetätigkeit trug er zur Verbreitung der 'Inventionsflöte' bei. Seine wenigen Kompositionen für die Flöte haben ihn kaum überlebt. Auch im Materiellen war Dulon ein erfolgreicher und kritisch denkender Instrumental-Künstler. Was er als Mensch unter besonderen Lebensbedingungen und als Künstler empfand und erlebte, hat er - teils sehr ins Einzelne gehend - niederschreiben lassen. Was bot und bietet er damit?

Dulon informiert über Risiken und Umstände der Reisetätigkeit eines Instrumentalvirtuosen, über Publikumsverhalten und Probleme der (damaligen) Konzertorganisation; er stellt die vielfältigen Abhängigkeiten eines reisenden Künstlers dar; Künstlerlaunen werden von ihm beschrieben; die Zustände in Städten und Gasthäusern behandelt er; er macht allgemeine Bemerkungen zu seinen Beobachtungen über Land und Leute, bei seinen Ansichten über die Engländer und deren Sprache verweilt er länger; der schnöde Mammon wird von ihm nicht verdrängt; über Ärzte hat er aus eigener Erfahrung seine sehr eigene Meinung; Empfindungen über das Blindsein versucht er wiederzugeben; über den Patriotismus stellt er eigene Betrachtungen an; auch Fürstengnade, Abendmahl, Gott und Unsterblichkeit sind Themen meist längerer 'Meynungs'-Äußerungen.

Von besonderer Bedeutung sind jene Eindrücke, welche berühmte Zeitgenossen, Musiker und Fachkollegen bei Dulon hinterließen; Flötenhistoriker finden interessante, ja einmalige Angaben über Professionelle und Liebhaber ihres Faches.

Die plaudernden Schilderungen Dulons sind mit zahlreichen bedenkenswerten Lebensweisheiten durchsetzt. Lassen wir einige dieser geisthaltigen 'Meynungen' auf uns wirken, ohne danach zu fragen, ob es selbstgedachte oder übernommene Sentenzen sein mögen:

Talente gewähren ihrem Besitzer
nur dann dauerhafte Vorteile,
wenn er mit demjenigen,
was er durch sie erwirbt,
haushälterisch zu Werke geht.[24]

Soweit kann der Eigendünkel
einen sonst verständigen Menschen bringen,
daß er bis zur lächerlichen Karikatur
herabsinkt.[25]

Wer da reist, um sein Brot zu erwerben,
und nicht zu der leichtsinnigen Klasse gehört,
der sieht erst auf seinen Vorteil
und dann auf sein Vergnügen.[26]

Als Reisende mußten Sie es doch wohl schon längst
voraus wissen,
daß man sich die Zuneigung der Briten
nur dann erwerben kann,
wenn man fähig ist,
ihnen in ihrer Mundart zu sagen,
daß sie die einzigen Beschützer der Künste und Wissenschaft sind
die es auf dem Erdenrunde gibt.[27]

Denn wirklich ist allzu große Nachgiebigkeit der Kinder
gegen Eltern
oftmals für jene von ebenso schlimmen Folgen,
als es der halsstarrige Ungehorsam nur immer sein kann.[28]

So mancher Redliche,
der in die große Welt trat
ohne die gehörige Erfahrung mitzubringen,
wurde durch allzufrühe Vertraulichkeit
ins Unglück gestürzt.[29]

Für den Künstler selbst
gibt es weder alte noch neue,
sondern nur gute und schlechte,
nützliche und schädliche Musik.[30]

*Echter Patriotismus
besteht mehr darin,
für das Vaterland tätig zu leben,
als sich für dasselbe
totschlagen zu lassen.*[31]

*Alle bekannten Religionsparteien in Europa
legen Gott das Prädikat
des Gnädigen und Barmherzigen bei,
und gleichwohl
kommen doch alle darin überein,
daß eben dieser gnädige und barmherzige Gott
jeden,
der nur ein Haar breit von dem abweicht,
was sie ihm zu glauben befehlen,
seiner Gerechtigkeit wegen
zu endlosen Qualen verdammen werde.*[32]

*Niemand,
der ein wenig Welterfahrung gesammelt hat,
wird leugnen,
daß die Moralität
unter den Priestern und Priesterinnen der Thalia
eben nicht
ihren Wohnsitz aufgeschlagen hat.*[33]

*Man fährt ja weit bequemer dabei,
wenn man ein Unternehmen in Gottes Namen beginnt,
als in seinem eigenen;
dort kann man,
wenn es fehlschlägt,
getrost unserm Herrngott alles zur Last legen;
hier aber ist man gezwungen,
sich die Schuld allein beizumessen.*[34]

*Torheit ist unstreitig eine Krankheit,
und eine wohl angebrachte Satyre
die beste Arzney dafür.*[35]

*Eine Freiheit,
die sich nicht auf die Ausübung erstreckt,
ist im Grunde soviel
als keine.*[36]

*Die allgemeine Erfahrung bestätigt leider,
daß Reichtum und Freigebigkeit
selten miteinander gepaart sind.*[37]

*Überhaupt glaube ich, daß der Geldverdienst
nicht gerade das einzige ist,
worauf es einem Künstler ankommen muß.*[38]

*Hast Du es als Künstler
zu einem gewissen Grad der Vollkommenheit gebracht,
so suche
es auch als Mensch dahin zu bringen.
Sorge dafür,
daß Deine Sitten, Dein Betragen, mit einem Wort:
Dein Menschenwert
Deinem künstlerischen gleichkommen möge.
Durch diesen erwirbst Du Ruhm und Geld,
durch jenen Achtung und Liebe.
Dieser öffnet Dir die Beutel,
jener die Herzen der Menschen.*[39]

*Edle Seelen
sind mit allen Menschen verwandt,
welche Hülfeleistung von ihnen bedürfen,
und nichts als die Unmöglichkeit
kann sich dieser Verwandtschaft
entgegensetzen.*[40]

3 Zur Entstehungs- und Druckgeschichte der Dulon'schen Lebenserinnerungen

Über die Entstehung des Manuskriptes von Dulons Selbstbiographie findet man in der Fachliteratur unterschiedliche Versionen: R.S. Rockstro, der sonst (fast) alles ganz genau wissen wollende englische Flötenlehrer und - historiker, weiß zu berichten, daß Dulon mit einem eigens für ihn erfundenen erhöhten Alphabet des damals sehr bekannten Petersburger Pädagogen C.H. Wolke gearbeitet habe;[41] Kölbel schreibt, Dulon habe seine Erinnerungen dem großen Dichter C.M. Wieland sozusagen in die Feder diktiert[42] (als ob dieser nichts Besseres zu tun hatte). - Beide Erklärungsversuche erweisen sich indessen als nicht stichhaltig.

Schon Schilling wußte zu berichten, daß sich Dulon 'in den müßigen Stunden ... fortwährend vorlesen ließ, so daß man ihn auch bei der schon erwähnten eminenten Stärke seines Gedächtnisses einen belesenen Mann nennen konnte. Eine besondere Vorliebe zeigte er dabei für Wielands Erzählungen, die er alle wörtlich auswendig wußte'.[43] Gerber gibt dafür ein konkretes Beispiel: 1795 erschien Wielands Verserzählung 'Die Wasserkufe'; Dulon behauptete imstande zu sein, 'wenn irgendeinmal alle Abdrucke derselben zugrunde gingen, selbige bis auf die letzte Silbe aus dem Kopfe wieder herzustellen'.[44] 'Die Wasserkufe' umfaßt in Wielands Gesamtausgabe, Band 12, Leipzig 1855, die Seiten 95 bis 126.

Dulon hatte schon Vorarbeiten geleistet, als er im September 1805 gelegentlich eines Konzertes in Weimar mit C.M. Wieland bekannt wurde und dieser aus Begeisterung für den Menschen und Künstler Dulon sich zur Revision und Herausgabe der Memoiren bereiterklärte.

Offenbar war es so, daß Dulon bereits um die Jahrhundertwende daranging, seiner 'Schwester Reinstein' Erinnerungen in die Feder zu diktieren; das Vorwort zu Band I ist nämlich datiert 'Stendal im Jahr 1802'. - Die A.M.Z. brachte im Februar 1803 den Hinweis, daß Dulon beabsichtige, seine Biographie in drei Bänden bei Vieweg in Braunschweig herauszugeben.[45] Im Mai 1803 steuerte Dulon selbst einen A.M.Z.-Brief über seine Absicht bei.[46]

Im Januar 1804 weiß die A.M.Z. zu berichten, daß Dulon 'mit der Beschreibung seines Lebens weit vorgerückt (sei)'.[47]

In das Stadium der Veröffentlichungsreife kam Dulons Werk aber erst mit und nach dem Treffen mit Wieland im September 1805, der die Verbindung zu dem Verleger (und seinem Schwiegersohn) Heinrich Geßner in Zürich herstellte, in dessen Verlag die beiden erschienenen Bände 1807 und 1808 herausgebracht wurden.

Einige erhaltene Briefe Wielands geben folgende Aufschlüsse:

1 Brief Wieland an Geßner vom 19.1.1806:[48]
Wieland übersendet 'endlich' eine leserliche Abschrift von einem Drittel des ersten Teiles der Biographie und schildert die Umstände der Übernahme seiner Funktion als Herausgeber sowie den (vorher nicht geahnten) Umfang seiner Inanspruchnahme; er empfiehlt das Erscheinen zur Ostermesse 1807.

2 Brief Wieland an Dulon vom 26.3.1806:[49]
Die Biographie sollte mit den beiden ersten Teilen zu Ostern 1807 erscheinen, der dritte zur Herbstmesse folgen. Wieland hatte viele Mühen mit der Bearbeitung des Manuskriptes, das 'über allen Begriff schlecht und fehlervoll geschrieben' war; deshalb 'ging es aber auch mit der Ausmistung dieses wahren Augias-Stalls etwas langsam her'. 'Aber der Gedanke, daß es Dulon sey, für welchen und aus Liebe zu welchem ich mich dieser Mühe unterzog, stärkte meine Geduld.'

3 Brief Wieland an Geßner vom 2.5.1806:[50]
Wieland äußert sich kurz zur Absicht Geßners, Dulons Werk in vier Bänden 'schon zur heurigen Jubiläumsmesse' zu bringen.

4 Brief Wieland an Dulon vom 22.1.1807:[51]
Wieland hat erst jetzt das Manuskript des dritten Teiles erhalten, das am 1.Oktober 1806 zur Post gegeben wurde. Er ist über Umfang (330 Seiten) und Handschrift erschrocken und empfiehlt, daß sein Schwiegersohn Geßner die Bearbeitung übernehmen möge, die er seines Alters und anderer Verpflichtungen wegen nicht mehr machen könne. Die Zeitumstände hätten überdies den Druck von Teil 1 und 2 aufgeschoben.

5 Brief Wieland an Dulon vom 23.11.1807:[52]
Auch Wieland erinnert sich gern an den 5.September (1805), als Dulon bei ihm und in seinem häuslichen Kreise feierte. - Geßner will Ostern 1808 wenigstens den 1. Teil der Biographie herausbringen. Wieland hat Geßner die Korrektur des 3. Teiles überlassen.

6 Brief Wieland an Dulon vom 19.8.1808:[53]
Wieland übersendet einen bedauerlichen Brief von Geßner. Er klagt über 'zunehmenden Verfall des Buchhandels'. Geßner bittet um Aufschub seiner Zahlungstermine.

Nach mehrjähriger Erkrankung starb Geßner, gerade 45 Jahre alt, im Jahre 1813.[54] Mit ihm erlosch der Verlag, und die Fortsetzung von Dulons Biographie war damit endgültig als undurchführbar besiegelt. Ob ein ungedruckter Teil der Biographie bei Geßner - oder sonstwo - verblieb und was damit geschah, das ist ungewiß.

Journal des Luxus und der Moden, September 1805, S. 634,635.

VI. Miscellen und Modenberichte.
Der Flötenspieler Dulon in Weimar.

Weimar d. 2 September 1805.
Diesen Abend gab der berühmte Flötenspieler Dulon im hiesigen geschmackvollen Schiesshaussaal ein Konzert in Anwesenheit des ganzen Hofes und einer grossen zahlreichen Versammlung. Von seinem Talent wurde in öffentlichen Blättern schon so oft und so viel gesprochen, dass es überflüssig sein würde, jetzt noch ein Wort zu seinem Lobe beizufügen. Hier nur von dem Eindrucke, den sein kunstreiches Spiel auf uns machte. — Seine fast unerreichbare Fertigkeit zeigte er abermals in den beiden Konzerten von Krommer und Müller (in Leipzig), ersteres aus G dur, letzteres aus D moll; deren wahren Charakter er mit ächtem Kennerohr aufgefasst hatte und meisterhaft durchführte. Allgemein fesselte uns sein, nicht mit eigner schwülstiger Fantasie überladener Vortrag, das mit weiser Vorsicht angebrachte Tempo rubato, das cresc. und decrescendo des schönen, sich immer gleichbleibenden Glockentons, den er bis zur äussersten Zartheit unserm getäuschten Ohr in ein Echo überführte. — Voll reiner Kunst und unübertreffbar war sein Staccato, die Doppelzunge in chromatischen Läufern, seine immer gleichbleibende Deutlichkeit in Behandlung der Passagen im pp wie im ff, eben so die Gleichförmigkeit der Töne, vom untersten bis zum höchsten.

Auch auf unser Gefühl wirkte er mächtig mit künstlerischer Zauberkraft, durch das ineinander Schmelzen und Durchziehen eines Tons in den andern. Sein in der geschmackvollen Kadenz im Konzert von Krommer passend angebrachter Schluss- oder Nachtigalltriller, den er richtig berechnet, nicht wie gewöhnlich, sondern den Hülfston mit dem zweiten Finger der rechten Hand gab, der stets wachsend und abnehmend bis zum morendo deutlich war, liess alle Möglichkeit dem göttlich beseelten Athem des Künstlers eine noch grössere Dauer und Stärke zu geben, hinter sich.

Um unser schon berauschtes Gefühl aufs höchste zu spannen, gab er uns als eigener Schöpfer, seine zarten Variationen über das bekannte Lied: ein freies Leben usw. Durch dies Alles erwarb sich Dulon bei uns allgemeinen Beifall und Bewunderung. Seiner Kunst vollkommen mächtig, lebt der des Augenlichts seit dem dritten Monat seiner Geburt beraubte Künstler ganz in der harmonischen Ideenwelt, und wirkt mit unbegränztem Geist auf das entzückte Herz und Ohr seiner Zuhörer.

Journal des Luxus und der Moden, Junius 1806, S. 355-357.

Der Flötenspieler Dulon in Halle.

Halle, den 7. März 1806.
Die Vorlesungen für dies Sommerhalbejahr, wurden durch ein öffentliches Konzert, das der so allgemein bekannte Virtuose auf der Flöte, Herr Dulon gab, auf eine eben so schöne als würdige Art eröffnet. Dulon blies zwei Konzerte von Müller und Hofmeister, und schloss mit den schönsten Variationen über ein bekanntes Volkslied. — Es war ein wehmütiger und rührender Anblick, als man den blinden Mann herbeiführte und vor die versammelte Menge hinstellte. Ach er kann das erfreuliche Licht des Tages nicht schauen; kann die tausendfachen

Schönheiten der jetzt neu belebten Natur nicht fühlen; konnte die Empfindungen des Entzückens und der Bewunderung von dem Gesichte seiner begeisterten Zuhörer nicht lesen! Und doch lag in seinen Mienen der Ausdruck eines stillen und ruhigen Gemüthes, eines freundlichen, zufriedenen Sinnes.

Dulon würde wahrscheinlich nie der grosse Künstler geworden sein, der er wirklich ist, wenn er die Welt mit allen ihren Disharmonieen und Bizarrerieen von Jugend auf gesehen hätte. Denn die wahre Musik kommt einzig aus einem reinen Herzen, und ist allein für's Ohr. — Die Nachtigall, wenn sie ihre lieblichsten flötendsten Töne hervorbringt, drückt die Augen fest zu, und vernimmt von alle dem nichts, was um sie her vorgeht. Eben so höre ich eine schöne Musik nicht anders als mit zugeschlossenen Augen, um mein ganzes Dasein auf den einzigen, reinen Genuss des Ohrs zu konzentrieren.

Ich will jeden sehen, sagt Nataliens Oheim in Göthe's Wilhelm Meister, mit dem ich reden soll, denn es ist ein einzelner Mensch, dessen Gestalt und Charakter die Rede wert oder unwert macht; hingegen wer mir singt (oder musiziert), soll unsichtbar sein, seine Gestalt soll mich nicht bestechen oder irre führen. Hier spricht nur ein Organ zum Organe, nicht der Geist zum Geiste, nicht eine tausendfältige Welt zum Auge, nicht ein Himmel zum Menschen — Indem sich das eingeschränkte Individuum, das die Musik hervorbringt, vor's Auge stellt, zerstört es den reinen Genuss der Allgemeinheit usw. — Alles dieses passt mit einigen Modificationen auch genau auf den Künstler.

Ueber Dulon's Spiel selbst, schreibe ich Ihnen nichts; schon viele Zeitschriften haben sich in Worten erschöpft, um einen Begriff von der Vortrefflichkeit seines Spiels zu geben. Aber die Musik ist keine Sprache, und Empfindungen lassen sich nicht in Worten ausdrücken. Wer vermag auch die leisen Uebergänge, von dem sanften Ausdrucke zarter Empfindungen bis zum kräftigen Vortrage hoher und starker Gefühle darzustellen? — Wer will den himmlischen Geist, den der grosse Künstler in einem schmelzenden Adagio aushaucht, auffassen? Wer kann das bald langsame, bald rasche Auf- und Niedersteigen, das Zusammenschmelzen und Wiederauflösen der Töne, und das daraus zusammengesetzte, vollendete Ganze durch Worte ausdrücken? — Nein, das alles will gehört und gefühlt sein. Hier ist die Redekunst ausser ihrem Gebiete. Es geht uns damit eben so, wie mit Schilderungen schöner Gegenden. Auch die glücklichsten Zeichnungen in treuen und kräftigen Zügen, die gelungensten Schilderungen, in einer lebendig darstellenden Sprache, können nur einen schwachen Schattenriss von den erhabenen Schauspielen und reizenden Ansichten der Natur geben. Sie können nur dazu dienen, Jemanden in jene Gegenden zurückzusetzen, die einst in entzückender Wirklichkeit vor seinen Augen lagen — so wie mir der Schattenriss den abwesenden Freund vor die Seele führt!
C.W.Sp.

Journal des Luxus und der Moden, Februar 1809, S. 108, 109.

Konzerte des Herrn Dulon und der Fräulein Therese v. Winkel in Weimar.

Wir haben vor kurzem in zwei Konzerten Gelegenheit gehabt, uns der Talente des bekannten blinden Flötenspielers, des Herrn Dulon, von neuem zu erfreuen.

Im ersten Konzert, am 27. Dezember 1808, trug Herr Dulon ein Konzert von Hoffmeister und eins von A.E. Müller in Leipzig mit vieler Fertigkeit und Präzision vor, und versicherte sich aufs neue, besonders durch die schöne Ausführung des letzten, des einstimmigen Beifalls der zahlreich versammelten Anwesenden.

Unsere brave Sängerin, Mad. Becker, geb. Ambrosch verschönerte diesen Abend durch eine glänzende Bravourarie von Mozart, worin sie Gelegenheit hatte, die Biegsamkeit und den Umfang ihrer Stimme hinlänglich zu zeigen. Herr Stromeyer entzückte uns durch den vortrefflichen Gesang einer Szene von Maurer, die dieser der Kunst so früh Entrissene, ganz für seine umfangreiche Stimme gesetzt hatte. Zuletzt spielte Herr Dulon einige artige Variationen, ohne weitere Begleitung, über Göthe's Lied: Da droben auf jenem Berge usw.

Im zweiten Konzerte, am 6. Januar 1809, hörten wir von Dulon eine der schönsten Flötenkompositionen von Müller (ich meine das Konzert aus F dur) und Variationen über ein polnisches Lied.

Ein Terzett von Cimarosa, gesungen von Dem. Jagemann, Dem. Hässler und Herrn Stromeyer und eine Bassarie von Mozart machten uns diesen Abend noch genussreicher.

Auch liess sich der erst kürzlich von Gotha zurückgekommene Herr Götze, ein junger talentvoller Violinspieler, mit einer Komposition seines Lehrers, Herrn Spohr's, hören und zeigte, dass er, seit wir ihn nicht hörten, beträchtliche Fortschritte gemacht habe. Möge er seinen Eifer nicht erkalten lassen, so wird er gewiss einst einen ehrenvollen Platz unter den besten Virtuosen dieses Instruments einnehmen.

Den Beschluss machten Variationen über Paesiello's bekanntes Nel cor piu non mi sento etc., gesungen von Dem. Jagemann und Herrn Stromeyer, geblasen von Herr Dulon; alle drei wetteiferten, ihre glänzenden Kunstfertigkeiten auf alle Art geltend zu machen.

Kaum war Dulon abgereist, als uns durch die Ankunft der aus Paris nach Dresden zurückkehrenden Fräulein Therese v. Winkel ein neuer Kunstgenuss bereitet ward; sie gab uns nämlich am 12. Januar eine Soirée de Musique und zeigte sich als eine sehr fertige, gewandte und oft sehr ausdrucksvolle Harfenspielerin. Vorzüglich sind ihr gelungen die Sonate von Marin und der Fandango mit Variationen von Dalvimare; in beiden benutzte sie die treffliche Pariser Pedalharfe von Erard meisterhaft. Sehr viel Interesse erregte die Hymne des Jon auf den Apoll von Reichardt, gesungen von Dem. Jagemann, und der vierstimmige Gesang aus dem Oratorio I Pellegrini von Naumann.

R.

Verwendete Abkürzungen

A.M.Z. Allgemeine Musikalische Zeitung, Leipzig, ab 1798.

NTL Ernst Ludwig Gerber, Neues historisch-biographisches Lexikon der Tonkünstler, 4 Bde, Leipzig 1812-1814.

EMW Gustav Schilling, Encyclopädie der gesamten musikalischen Wissenschaften oder Universallexikon der Tonkunst, 6 Bde, Stuttgart 1835-1838

MGG Die Musik in Geschichte und Gegenwart. Allgemeine Enzyklopädie der Musik (Hrsg. Friedrich Blume), 14 u. 2 Suppl.-Bde, Kassel und Basel 1949-1979.

NDB Neue Deutsche Biographie. Herausgegeben von der Historischen Kommission bei der Bayerischen Akademie der Wissenschaften, Berlin, ab 1953.

Anmerkungen

1 genauer Titel: Dülons des blinden Flötenspielers Leben und Meynungen von ihm selbst bearbeitet. Herausgegeben von C.M. Wieland. Zürich, bey Heinrich Geßner.
Erster Theil 1807 (künftig abgekürzt T.I)
Zweyter Theil 1808 (künftig abgekürzt T.II).
Beide Teile enthalten kein Inhaltsverzeichnis; dieses sei hier mit leicht gekürzten Kapitelüberschriften gegeben:

Teil 1
Vorbericht, S.3
Kap. 1 Ursprung der Familie S.15
Kap. 2 Geburt und Erblindung; über Augenärzte S.20
Kap. 3 Über Blindheit; Trostgründe; über Gefühl und Gedächtnis S.29
Kap. 4 Kinderjahre S.46
Kap. 5 Unterricht in französischer Sprache S.58
Kap. 6 Erster Flötenunterricht S.63
Kap. 7 Reise in die Schweiz; fehlgeschlagene Kur eines wirklichen Augenarztes S.71
Kap. 8 Komponiersucht S.76
Kap. 9 Erster Auftritt; Unterricht im Generalbaß S.80
Kap. 10 Bekanntschaft mit Herrn Zink S.88
Kap. 11 Nötige Vorerinnerungen S.92
Kap. 12 Erste musikalische Wanderungen S.98
Kap. 13 Dritte musikalische Wanderung; über das Wort Gnade S.120
Kap. 14 Vierte musikalische Wanderung S.141
Kap. 15 Anfang größerer Reisen S.192
Kap. 16 In Potsdam und Berlin S.214
Kap. 17 Über den Sinn des Geruchs; über Patriotismus; Weiterreise S.225
Kap. 18 In Schwedt; über Schauspiel S.256
Kap. 19 In Stettin; über Freunde S.282
Kap. 20 In Greifswald und Stralsund S.297
Kap. 21 Von Stralsund bis Bremen; Winke für reisende Tonkünstler S.314
Kap. 22 Über Reisen und Konzertieren 'in Compagnie'; Weiterreise; über den Einfluß der

Jahreszeiten auf die Musik S.362
Kap. 23 Musik ist keine freie Kunst; Reise bis Magdeburg; über Wohltaten im stillen S.411

Teil 2
Kap. 1 Reise mit Vater und Bruder (bis Leipzig) S.3
Kap. 2 Familienreise von Magdeburg bis Mainz S.49
Kap. 3 Reise in die Schweiz, Rückkehr nach Mainz S.95
Kap. 4 In Mainz und Frankfurt; neue Pläne; Reise bis Wesel S.143
Kap. 5 In Kleve; allgemeine Betrachtungen S.161
Kap. 6 Reisen am Niederrhein S.182
Kap. 7 Familienbegebenheiten; in Amsterdam S.206
Kap. 8 'Mein guter Genius'; an deutsche Patrioten S.220
Kap. 9 Über Holland und seine Bewohner S.228
Kap. 10 Weiterreise nach England; Ankunft in London S.246
Kap. 11 In London S.295
Kap. 12 Rückkehr ins Vaterland S.338
Kap. 13 In Köln und Münster; Aufnahme in die christlich-reformierte Gemeine und Gedanken darüber; in Hildesheim und Hannover S.380
Kap. 14 In Preussisch-Minden; über Empfehlungs-Schreiben S.416

2 Siehe Rezension in A.M.Z. 1809, 245; EMW I, 507.

3 Siehe Karl Ventzke, Dr. J.J.H. Ribock (1743-1785). Ein Beitrag zur Entwicklungsgeschichte der Querflöte. In: Tibia (Celle) 2/76, 65-71.

4 Siehe Fritz Demmler, Johann George Tromlitz (1725-1805). Ein Beitrag zur Entwicklung der Flöte und des Flötenspiels. Diss. FU Berlin 1961; Karl Ventzke, Frühe Nachrichten über Flöten und Kompositionen von Johann George Tromlitz. In: Tibia 2/78, 105-106.

5 NTL I, 949.

6 EMW I, 508.

7 NDB IV, 187.

8 A.M.Z. Okt. 1799, 54.

9 A.M.Z. Sept. 1800, 879.

10 Herausgegeben von Friedrich Justin Bertuch (1747-1822) in Weimar.

11 Stadtarchiv Würzburg an den Verfasser 16.1.1974.

12 Wie 11.

13 In: Caecilia, Mainz, Bd. I/1824, 58.

14 NDB IV, 187.

15 T.II, 225.

16 T.II, 394.

17 T.II, 221-224.

18 Für diesen Hinweis danke ich Herrn Dr. Lenz Meierott, Gerbrunn bei Würzburg, mitgeteilt am 1.6.1975; danach hat Dulon mehrfach und regelmäßig (auch vor seinem Umzug nach Würzburg) in Würzburg konzertiert, so wird z.B. ausführlich in der Fränkisch-Würzburgischen Chronik vom 23.11.1811 über ein Dulon-Konzert am 31.Oktober 1811 in Würzburg berichtet.

19 Siehe MGG 3, 924.

20 A. Ritt wirkte von 1792 bis zu seinem Tode 1799 in Petersburg.

21 A.M.Z. Jan. 1809, 241-249 und 257-262.

22 EMW I, 509.

23 NTL I, 949.

24 T.II, 116.

25 T.II, 130.

26 T.II, 325.

27 T.II, 319.

28 T.II, 367.

29 T.II, 389.

30 T.I, 69.

31 T.I, 235.

32 T.I, 140.

33 T.I, 278.

34 T.II, 53.

35 T.I, 343.

36 T.I, 417.

37 T.II, 71.

38 T.I, 156.

39 T.I, 96.

40 T.II, 8.

41 Richard S. Rockstro, A Treatise on the Construction, the History and the Practice of the Flute ..., 2nd Edition, London 1928, 569.

42 Herbert Kölbel, Von der Flöte. Brevier für Flötenspieler. Köln und Krefeld 1951, 165.

43 EMW I, 508/509.

44 NTL I, 949.

45 A.M.Z. Febr. 1803, 374/375.

46 Intelligenzblatt zur A.M.Z. Mai 1803.

47 A.M.Z. Jan. 1804, 268.

48 Im Deutschen Literaturarchiv/Schiller-Nationalmuseum, Marbach am Neckar.

49 Wie 48.

50 Abgedruckt in: Der Türmer, Jahrgang 9/1906, 23.

51 Im Goethe- und Schiller-Archiv, Weimar (NFG/GSA).

52 In der Bodleian Library, Oxford, MS Montagu d. 20.

53 In der Landesbibliothek Dortmund.
Ich danke den unter 48-53 genannten Institutionen für die Zugänglichmachung der Briefe.

54 Stadtarchiv Zürich an den Verfasser 28.6.1974; danach war Heinrich Geßner, geb. 1768 in Zürich, der jüngere Sohn des berühmten Idyllendichters Salomon Geßner (1730-88). Er heiratete 1795 Charlotte Wieland aus Weimar (1776-1816). Geßner verlegte auch mehrere Werke des berühmten Erziehers und Sozialreformers Johann Heinrich Pestalozzi (1746-1827).

Weiteres Schrifttum über Dulon:

Reinhold Sietz, Der Flötenvirtuose Friedrich Ludwig Dülon. In: Die Musikforschung VII/1954, 460-463.

Hans Joachim Moser, Blinde Musiker aus 7 Jahrhunderten. Hamburg 1956.

Bilitis:
eine beinahe vergessene Liebe von Claude Debussy

Karl Lenski

*Des amours de Bilitis il reste aussi une
petite flûte. Je ne sais si elle suspendrait les
rivières d' Arcadie; mais elle suffit à excuser une
vie un peu en dehors de la morale vulgaire.*

Pierre Louÿs, *Vie de Bilitis* (1894)

Im Jahre 1891 machte der 29-jährige Debussy im Pariser *Cabaret du Clou*, Treffpunkt vieler Künstler, die Bekanntschaft eines jungen Dichters, Pierre Louÿs. Dieser hatte folgende, einem Manifest gleichende Sätze geschrieben: 'Wer wird als erster ein Gedicht so genau zu rhythmisieren wissen, dass der Komponist es nur noch zu transkribieren und zu orchestrieren braucht, gewissermassen nur als Ausführender; wer wird so endgültige Dichtungen schaffen, dass die Musik zu jedem Gesang nur noch die Andeutung einer Begleitung hinzuzufügen braucht...?'[1] Die Ideen Pierre Louÿs' wirkten auf den jungen Debussy überaus fruchtbar, beeinflussten wesentlich sein kompositorisches Schaffen, selbst noch zu einem Zeitpunkt, als die tiefe, bereichernde Freundschaft dieser beiden Künstler nur noch in der Erinnerung beider bestand! Es war Pierre Louÿs, dem Claude Debussy seine eigentliche intellektuelle Bildung zu verdanken hatte, wie es Léon Vallas, der getreue Biograph von Achille-Claude, uns so liebevoll und überzeugend mitteilt.[2]
Es war auch der Dichter, der den noch unbekannten Herrn De Bussy (sic) - *L'Après-Midi d'un Faune* entstand erst ein bis zwei Jahre später und verhalf mit der Pariser Uraufführung am 22.12.1894 Debussy zum 'Durchbruch' - mit anderen Dichtern und Malern, den 'Symbolisten' (der Begriff war noch ganz jung und unbelastet) in Berührung brachte und es ihm ermöglichte, in den 'heiligen' Kreis des damaligen Dichterpapstes, Stéphane Mallarmé, aufgenommen zu werden - als einziger Musiker! - und an den wöchentlich stattfindenden Poesieabenden teilzunehmen, und somit selbst zum 'homme de lettres' zu werden; Mallarmé, der später (1895) Debussy, wohl als Dank für dessen 'Übersetzung' seiner eigenen unsterblichen Faun-Dichtung diese Verse widmete:

*Sylvain d'haleine première
Si ta flûte a réussi
Ouïs toute la lumière
Qu'y soufflera Debussy.*

Zwanzig Jahre liegen zwischen dem Erscheinen der *Chansons de Bilitis* von Pierre Louÿs und den *Six Epigraphes Antiques* von Claude Debussy. Im Dezember 1894 - im gleichen Monat kam *L'Après-Midi* zur Aufführung - veröffentlichte Pierre Louÿs in *L'Art Indépendant* als 'Übersetzung aus dem Griechischen' den Gedichtzyklus *Bilitis*, in dem die gleichnamige antike

Schönheit besungen wird. Dem Vorwort zufolge lebte Bilitis im sechsten vorchristlichen Jahrhundert, die *Chansons* waren als Erinnerung an sie in ihren Grabstein graviert, erst kürzlich entdeckt von einem deutschen Gelehrten... Schon sehr bald nach dem Erscheinen der *Chansons de Bilitis* entpuppte sich die 'Übersetzung' als harmlose Täuschung; um den Spass komplet zu machen, sandte Louÿs sein Werk einem angesehenen Professor; der Lehrer dankte ihm höflich und fügte hinzu, er habe *Bilitis* schon lange vor ihm studiert!... der Dichter war Pierre Louÿs in höchsteigener Person.

Drei Werke von Claude Debussy basieren sich auf dieser pseudogriechischen Poesie: *Trois Chansons de Bilitis* (1897) für Sopran und Klavier, *Les Chansons de Bilitis* (1900), einer wenig bekannten Szenenmusik für Sprecher, zwei Flöten, zwei Harfen und Celesta[3] und schliesslich *Six Epigraphes Antiques* (1914) für Klavier zu vier Händen, denen Debussy noch eine Version für Klavier solo folgen liess.

Beinahe gänzlich versunken in *Pelléas et Mélisande* - wir wissen, welche Qualen ihm seine einzige Oper bereitete - entstanden im Frühjahr 1897 die *Trois Chansons de Bilitis*: *La Flûte de Pan*, *La Chevelure* - Jankélévitch stellte Parallelen zwischen diesem Chanson und dem Anfang von *Pelléas* (Mélisande: *Je me suis enfui*) fest - und *Le Tombeau des naïades*. 'Drei Chansons, drei fleckenlose Partituren, wunderbar eingestimmt auf die sinnliche Kunst und den deliziösen Paganismus von Pierre Louÿs', wo Debussy 'absolute Meisterschaft' erreicht, 'Höhepunkt der *art debussiste*', wie Léon Vallas voll Bewunderung schreibt.[4] Die Aufführung der *Trois Chansons de Bilitis* scheint nicht ohne Schwierigkeiten vonstatten gegangen zu sein - wohl des für die Zeit 'gewagten' Textes und der äusserst hohen künstlerischen Ansprüche wegen, die Debussy an den Sänger stellt - sie erlebten erst drei Jahre nach ihrer Entstehung ihre Uraufführung: am 17. März 1900 in der *Societé National* mit der Sängerin Blanche Marot und dem Komponisten am Klavier.

In einem Brief vom 25. Oktober 1900 erbittet Pierre Louÿs die Mitarbeit seines Freundes, um eine Begleitmusik zu der rezitierten und gemimten *Bilitis* zu schreiben, die Fernand Samuel, Direktor der *Variétés*, verlangt hatte: 'Hast Du einen genügend freien Kopf, um acht Seiten Geigen, Pausen und Blechakkorde zu schreiben, die einen sogenannten *Kunsteindruck* in den *Variétés* machen, ohne den armen Direktor schon vorher zum Heulen zu bringen?' Debussy akzeptiert und schreibt am 15. Januar 1901: 'Ich lege die letzte Hand an Bilitis..., wenn ich mich so ausdrücken darf.'[5] Die Uraufführung findet schon drei Wochen später statt, am 7. Februar, jedoch nicht in den *Variétés*, sondern im Festsaal des *Journal*. Die 'acht Seiten Geigen' - wohl die 'Pausen' - die 'Blechakkorde' scheinen Debussy nicht angestanden zu haben; er schrieb einige Blätter deliziöser Szenenmusik für die aparte Besetzung mit zwei Flöten, zwei Harfen und Celesta, zwölf Melodramen, kleine 'bijoux', äusserst kühn in ihrer Konzentriertheit und in der Art der Behandlung der poetischen Idee. Wie hatte Debussy noch auf die Frage seines alten Kompositionslehrers Ernest Guiraud, welcher Poet ihm denn wohl ein Gedicht liefern könne, geantwortet? 'Derjenige, der die Dinge halb sagt, der mir erlaubt, meine Träume mit den seinen zu vereinigen, der sich Gestalten ausmalt, deren Geschichte und deren Verbleib zeitlos und ohne Ort sind, der mich nicht despotisch zwingt, eine bestimmte *Inszenierung* zu gebrauchen, und der mir die Freiheit zugesteht, hie und da mehr *Kunst* (Genie) zu haben als er und seinem Werk letzte Vollendung zu geben... Jede musikalische Entwicklung, die nicht vom Wort her gerechtfertigt wird, ist falsch... Ich träume von Gedichten, die mich nicht zwingen, zu lange und zu schwere Akte zu schreiben; die mir mobile Szenen bescheren, verschieden nach Ort und Charakter; wo die Gestalten nicht diskutieren, sondern Leben und Schicksal unterliegen.'[6]

Pablo Picasso, *Flötenspieler und sitzende Frau*.

Pierre Louÿs

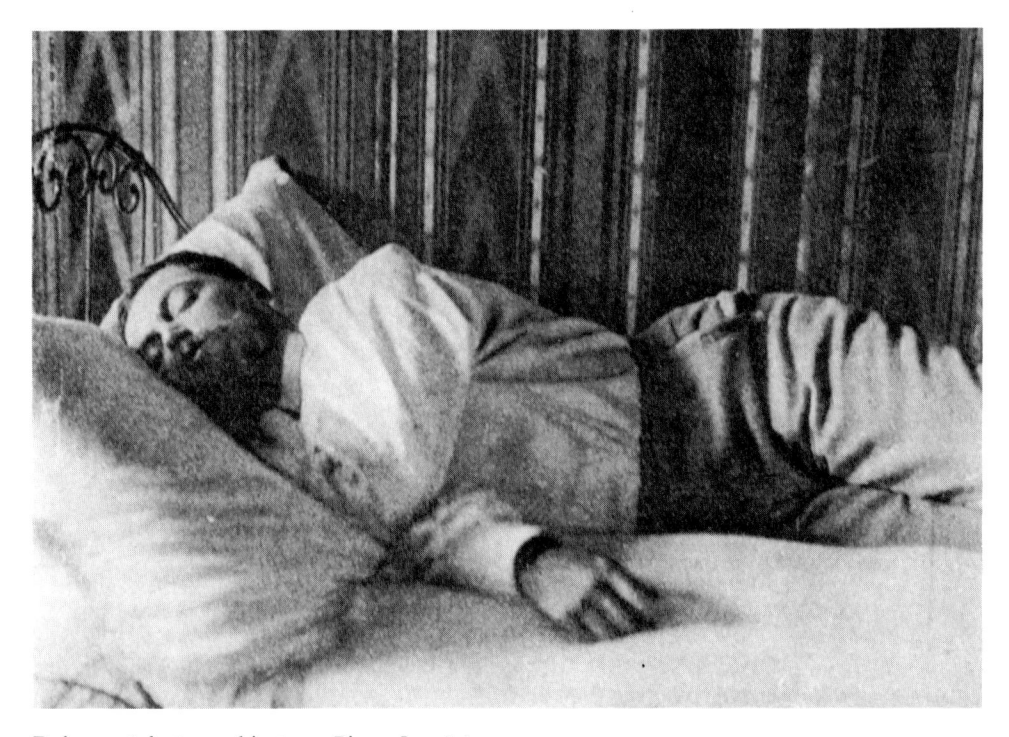

Debussy (photographiert von Pierre Louÿs)

Dieses sind präzise Sätze, beinahe prophetisch in ihrer Tragweite. In diesen Sätzen, geschrieben 1889, spiegelt sich die gesamte Ästhetik von *Pelléas* wieder.

De la musique avant toute chose,
Et pour cela préfère l'Impair
Plus vague et plus soluble dans l'air,
Sans rien en lui qui pèse ou qui pose.

Il faut aussi que tu n'ailles point
Choisir tes mots sans quelque méprise:
Rien de plus cher que la chanson grise
Où l'Indécis au Précis se joint.

C'est des beaux yeux derrière des voiles,
C'est le grand jour tremblant de midi
C'est par un ciel d'automne attiédi,
Le bleu fouillis des claires étoiles!

Car nous voulons la Nuance encor,
Pas la Couleur, rien que la nuance!
Oh! la nuance seule fiance
Le rêve au rêve et la flûte au cor! ...

Paul Verlaine, *Jadis et naguère* (1884)

Die Uraufführung der *Chansons de Bilitis* von Pierre Louÿs und Claude Debussy kannte zwar einen lebhaften Erfolg - die 'lebenden' Bilder wurden von P. Louÿs' eigener Hand geleitet vor einer Zuhörerelite, die sich - schenken wir der Rezension vom 8. Februar 1901 vom *Journal* Glauben - in 'reine paradisische Zeiten' zurückversetzt fühlten - es blieb jedoch bei dieser einzigen Aufführung. Erst ein halbes Jahrhundert später, im Jahre 1954, unternahm Pierre Boulez den Versuch, die in Vergessenheit geratene *Bilitis* wieder zum Leben zu erwecken; er rekonstruierte an Hand der *Six Epigraphes Antiques* aus dem Jahre 1914 die verlorengegangene Celestastimme und führte das Stück in der Konzertreihe von *Domaine Musical* auf.

Zwischen der *Szenenmusik,* die insgesamt 12 Nummern zählt, und den *Six Epigraphes Antiques*[7] besteht ein direkter inhaltlicher und thematischer Zusammenhang, wie aus folgendem vergleichenden Schema deutlich wird:

Epigraphes: I
Pour invoquer Pan, dieu du vent d'été
Modéré - dans le style d'une pastorale
primo

Szenenmusik: I
Chant pastoral
Modéré
Flöte 1 solo

Epigraphes: II
Pour un tombeau sans nom
Triste et lent
primo

Szenenmusik: VII
Le tombeau sans nom
Triste et lent
Flöte 1 solo

Epigraphes: II
comme une plainte lointaine
primo

Szenenmusik: VIII
Les courtisanes égyptiennes
Assez animé
Flöte 1

Epigraphes: III
Pour que la nuit soit propice
Lent et expressif
primo & secondo in Oktaven

Szenenmusik: IV
Chanson
Lent et expressif
Flöte 1 & 2 in Oktaven

Epigraphes: IV
Pour la danseuse aux crotales
Andantino (souple et sans rigueur)
primo

Szenenmusik: X
La danseuse aux crotales
Modéré (tempo rubato)
Flöte 1 → 2

Epigraphes: V
Pour l'Egyptienne
Très modéré
primo

Szenenmusik:
kommt hier in dieser Form nicht vor; Titel von *Epigraphes* weist jedoch nach Nr. VIII aus Szenenmusik *Les courtisanes égyptiennes*

Epigraphes: VI
Pour remercier la pluie au matin
Modérément animé
secondo

Szenenmusik: XII
La pluie au matin
Modéré
Flöte 1 & 2 unisono

Das Material der *Six Epigraphes Antiques* besteht etwa zu zwei Dritteln aus der Urfassung der *Chansons de Bilitis*; etwa ein Drittel weist zwar keinen direkten thematischen Zusammenhang mit diesen auf, Debussy komponiert jedoch deutlich den poetischen Inhalt der *Chansons* aus, was auch sichtlich durch quasi Strophen-Zäsuren und erklärende Zusätze wie zum Beispiel 'comme une plainte lointaine' in Nr. II oder 'doux et monotone' im Regenmotiv aus Nr. VI zu Tage tritt. Im sechsten Epigraph entfernt der Komponist sich am weitesten von der Urfassung - Debussys endgültiger Abschied von *Bilitis*, die ihn beinahe zwanzig Jahre lang beschäftigte?

Anmerkungen

1 Zitiert nach Juan Allende-Blin, *Claude Debussy: Scharnier zweier Jahrhunderte* in Musik-Konzepte: *Claude Debussy*, München, 1981.

2 Léon Vallas, *Achille-Claude Debussy*, Paris, 1944.

3 Die Celestastimme ist leider verlorengegangen. Die verbleibenden Instrumentalstimmen bewahrt heute die Nationalbibliothek in Paris. Pierre Boulez rekonstruierte 1954 die fehlende Celestapartie und führte das Werk in der Konzertreihe von *Domaine musical* auf. Rudolf Escher (1912-1980) unternahm ebenfalls einen bemerkenswerten Rekonstruktionsversuch und liess *Bilitis* 1972 in Amsterdam in *De Suite* mit einem ad hoc-Ensemble unter der Leitung von Ed Spanjaard aufführen. Das handschriftliche Material dieser Fassung bewahrt Donemus in Amsterdam. 1971 besorgte Arthur Hoérée eine Rekonstruktion für den Verlag Jobert, Paris.

4 l.c. S. 106.

5 In *Correspondance de C. Debussy et P. Louÿs*, Paris 1945.

6 In Paul Landormy *La Musique Française. De Franck à Debussy*, Paris 1943.

7 Der Autor dieser Zeilen hat den Versuch unternommen, die sechs *Bilitis* - Gesänge an Hand der *Six Epigraphes Antiques* für Flöte und Klavier einzurichten; diese Ausgabe wird im Herbst 1984 bei Universal Edition in Wien erscheinen.

De musicq lievende werd bekend gemaekt...

Rineke Smilde

Een keuze uit berichten over fluitisten, fluiten en fluitmuziek die tussen 1740 en 1760 verschenen zijn in de *Amsterdamsche Courant*.

30 januari 1742

> Maho, zal Woensdag den 31 January, Concert geeven in de Son op den Nieuwendyk, alwaer hy zig op de Fluyt Travers met Concerten en Solos van zyn Compofitie zal hooren laten. De Loten zyn te bekomen in de Stad Lion in de Nes, en in de Son op den Nieuwendyk, 2 gulden het Lot.

Over het leven van Antonio (Antoine) Mahaut (Mahault, Mahout) is weinig bekend. Aangenomen wordt dat hij van ca. 1740 tot 1760 in Amsterdam heeft gewoond. Dit bericht is een aanwijzing dat hij in deze periode ook als fluitist optrad.
In de herberg 'De Zon' werden regelmatig concerten gegeven. Aankondigingen verschijnen over optredens door o.a. Hellendaal (1743), Veracini (1746) en de gebroeders Graf (1751).

5 mei 1742

> Jan van Heerde, Muficael Inftrumentmaker en Vakoper in de Warmroesftraet tot Amfterdam, maekt bekent, dat door hem is gemaekt en by hem te bekomen, zekere Fluyt Travers, die men hoog en laeg kan ftellen, met het zelve gemak en accurateheid als men een Fiool doet.

In de volgende krant (8 mei 1742) verschijnt de advertentie weer, nu met de toevoeging 'zonder van middenstukken te veranderen'.

31 december 1743

> By J. N. Batailhey Boekverkoper op de Beursfluys t'Amfterd., is te bekomen, XII Sonate per Flauto Traverfiere Solo e' Baffo Continuo Opera Prima fol. a f 5 : 5. Sei Sonate a Tre Due Flauti o Due Violini Col Baffo, Da Signore Di Granom Gentilhuomo Ingelefe Opera Seconda fol. a f 3 : 5. : Deze twee Werken zyn gemaekt door de voornaemfte Liefhebber van de Dwarsfluyt, waer van zyn weerga in geheel Europa niet is bekend ; en zyn mede te bekomen in 's Hage by F. H. Scheurleer, Leyden C. Haak, Utregt G. Muller : By den zelve zyn nog te bekomen, Etrennes Mignones van Parys, voor 't jaer 1744, in allerhande Bantjes,

16 juli 1744

> PIETRO LOCATELLI woond t'Amft. op de Princegragt 't derde huys van de Leydfe Kruysftraet, verkoopt deze volgende Werken van zyn Compofition, gedrukt op eyge koften met Privilegie van de Ed. Gr. Mog. Heeren Staeten van Holland en Weft-Friesl.; Opera Ottava, X, Sonate, VI. à Violino Solo, é Baffo, é IV. à tré, tot 7 gl. ; als mede Opera Seconda, XII. Sonate à Flauto Traverfiere Solo, é Baffo,tot 6 gl. Opera Quinta VI. Sonate à Due Flauti Traverfieri é Baffo,tot 6 gl. : Opera Sefta XII. Sonate à Violino Solo,é Baffo, 6 gl.

Op 28 juni 1746 adverteert Locatelli nogmaals met deze werken. Hij deelt mee dat hem op 12 mei 1746 weer een drukprivilege is verleend voor 15 jaar.

115

24 oktober 1744

Men adverteert aen alle Heeren en Dames, en Liefhebbers van de Muficq, dat op aenftaende Dingsdag zynde den 27 October, door J. C. Richter, een Concert in 't Wapen van Embden op de Nieuwendyk, 's avonds ten 6 uuren zal gehouden werden, om zig te laten horen op Baffon en Flauto Piccolo: 't Biljet is 2 gulden, en zyn in 't Wapen van Embden te bekomen.

27 mei 1745

Aen de Liefhebbers van de Muzicq werd bekend gemaekt, dat onder de hand te koop is, en fo niet onder de hand verkogt werd, dat dan publyk verkogt zal werden, een beroemde Bibliotheek van Muzicq, beftaende in een generaele verzamelinge van allerly zoorten, fo van Vocale als Inftrumentaele gedrukte Muzicq-ftukken, benevens een groote quantiteyt der raerffe Manufcripten, alle van de beroemfte Meefters in Europa bekend zyn, keurlyk en welgeconditioneert, zedert 50 jaeren met zeer veel moyte en groote koften by een vergadert; nagelaten door de Heer en Mr. Jurianus van der Koft: Iemant genegeen zynde deeze confiderable Collectie te kopen, of de Catalogus daer van door den Overleedenen eygenhandig gefchreeven, behelzende meer als 7000 nommers te hebben, en de Muzicaele Inftrumenten te zien, addrefferen zig te Delft ten huyze van Mejuffr. de Wed. J. van der Koft op de Lakegragt. De Liefhebbers welke eenige Muzicq van den Overleedenen mogten onder zig hebben, werden verzogt dezelve fpoedig wederom te bezorgen.
G. F. Witvogel, heeft doen drukken J. Nozeman Opera Quinta 6 Sonata Solos voor de Violon Cello f 3 : 10 ft. 6 Duetten voor de Dwarsfluyt van Gio Battifta Patoni f 3. Zani Opera Seconda 12 Concerten voor de Violin f 12. D. Kelner Korte en Grondige Onderrigtinge van de Baffus Continuus, en uyt het Hoogduyts vertaelt door G. Havingha Organift te Alkmaer f 3 : 6 ft.; en zyn meede te bekomen 's Hage Selhof, Leyden Hack en Utregt Muller. By gem. Witvogel zyn te koop allerbefte Italiaenfe Fiool en Bas-Snaeren.
Pieter Keerman Orgel en Clavecimbaelmaker, maekt bekent, dat hy is gaen woonen op May 1745, in de Lange Leydfe Dwarsftraet tuffchen de Spiegelgragt en Kruysftraet over Vreedenburg; dat by hem te bekomen is een oud Orgel, bequaem in een Roomfche Kerk of Huys te gebruyken, met 5 en 1 helf Regifters, en een Blaesbalg zeer gemaklyk te behandelen: Ook zyn by hem te huur en te koop Oude Clavecimbaels van Rukkers, Couchet en andere Brabantfe Meefters.

Met duetten van Patoni werd ook geadverteerd in de Amsterdamsche Courant van 28 november 1744. Onder een andere advertentie werd vermeld: 'N.B. By gem. Boekverkoper (Olofsen in de Gravestraat te Amsterdam) als meede by Joh. Fred. Groneman Muzicqmeester, zullen in 't kort te bekomen zijn, Duetten voor de Viool en Dwarsfluyt, van den grooten Muzicqmeester Gio. Battista Patoni, voor 3 gulden compleet, op extra fraey papier.'

8 februari 1746

Op heeden geeft JOH. FRED. GRONEMAN, onder zyn opzigt, en A. OLOFSEN Boekverkoper in de Graveftraet, als meede by die der Buytenfteden by 't open water uyt: de 6 Sonaten Trioos, voor 2 Vioolen en 2 Dwarsfluyten, met dubbelde Baffen; door den ervaren Muziek-meefter Ant. Retzel; voor drie gulden.

4 februari 1747

t' Amfterd. werd by Joh. Fred. Groneman en A. Olofsen uytgegeven, de Mufiek-werken van Giufeppe Jozzi, 8 Sonaten voor het Clavier, a 3 guld. De Triôs van Pyanthanida voor de viool, f 5 : 5. De Triôs van Retzel voor Dwarsfluyt en Viool, f 3. De Duetten van Patroni voor de Dwarsfluyt en Viool, f 1 : 10. De Minuetten en Contradanffen van Duni, 1 gl. De Triôs en Solôs van Granom voor de Dwarsfluyt, ieder f 6 : 12. Als meede in 't kort de 6 Concerten van Retzel, die by ieder Concert zullen uytgegeven werden.

14 november 1747

t' Amfterd. by Joh. Côvens de Jonge op de Vygendam, zyn te bekomen, de Gereformeerde en Lutherfe Pfalmen voor het Clavier, door G. F. Witvogel, ieder a 6 guld. Canzonetten van de Fefch 50 ft. De Solos van Teffarini 5 guld. Van Geminiani 5 guld. voor de Viool. De Solos van Quants 3 guld. Van Santis 5 guld. Van de Fefch 50 ft. Weideman 4 guld. voor de Dwarsfluyt. De Duetten van Leclair voor de Viool 3 guld. Divertiffements voor twee Dwarsfluyten 2 guld. De Trios van de Fefch 6 guld. Teffarini 4 guld. voor de Dwarsfluyt. Sinfonie van Haffe 6 guld. Idem van Temanza 5 guld. Concerten van Santis 3 guld. Van Tartini 9 guld. Van Zani 10 en 12 guld. Voor de Viool van Haffe voor de Dwarsfluyt 6 guld. Pieces Choifies pour le Claveffin 50 ft. Hendel 62 Variations 50 ft. Sonata 14 ft. Capricia 18 ft. Prelude 14 ft. Fantafie 18 ft. Sentes van de Boek 24 ft. Kirchhof A. B. C. Muficael 2 guld. Scarlatti 30 Sonaten 6 gul. Geilfus 6 Sonatines 4 guld. Menuetten van Geminiani 30 ft. Guiftini 12 Sonaten 5 guld. Sonaten van Hafle 1 guld. Nozeman 24 Paftorellas 4 guld., alle voor 't Clavier.

2 januari 1749

Jan Fredrik en A. Groeneman, zullen op heeden Concert houden in 't Logement het Keyzershof en 't Wapen van Embden, op den Nieuwendyk t' Amft. 's avonds ten 6 uuren, de Lootjes zyn in 't voorn. Logement voor 1 gl. te bekomen. De voorn. Groeneman zal 12 Solos van differente Autheurs by intekening drukken, voor de Viool of Dwarsfluyt, de intekening is 4 gulden, en zullen naderhand niet minder als 6 guld. te bekomen zyn; die geneegen is in te tekenen kan zig by gemelde adrefferen.

116

16 oktober 1749

t'Amsterdam by J. Covens Junior, Boekverkoper op de hoek van de Vygendam en Warmoesstraet, is gedrukt en werd uytgegeven: VI Sonaten a tre due Violini, o due Flauti Traversi, Violoncello, e Basso Continuo Opera Secunda da A. Retzel; als mede de Musicq van Witvogel, en van le Cene en Roger.

Zes jaar daarvoor, op 24 november 1743 maakte de boekverkoper E.J. de la Coste bekend dat hij de nalatenschap van 'Muzyk-Werken' van Roger en Le Cène had bemachtigd. Hij kondigde aan de werken die op dat moment 'onder de Pers' waren te zullen uitgeven. Daarbij was o.a. van Ferrandini: 'Opera prima, Libro Secondo, à flauto Traversiero Solo, ƒ 4,–'. Op 17 september 1746 werd een openbare verkoping aangekondigd van de nalatenschap van de uitgever Witvogel.

13 juli 1751

Mr. Ciprutini zal op Donderdag den 15 July, 's avonds ten 6 uuren, t'Amsterdam in de Zon op de Nieuwendyk Concert houden; de Loorjes zyn aldaer, en by hem op de eerste Weesperstraet a ƒ 1-10 te bekomen, met een Dame vry.
JOAN FREDRIK GRONEMAN zal morgen wederom Vocaal en Instrumentael Concert geven in de Vauxhall op de Weg van den Overtoom, zullende beginnen ten half vyf uuren, ook zullen zig verscheide VIRTUOSEN laten horen, en zal driemael in de week 's Maendags, Woensdags en Saturdags daer mede continueeren; ook zal voor een premie van ƒ 25, een Mast beklommen werden, en kunnen die geene die daer toe bekwaem zyn zig by hem adresseeren.

Groneman adverteert tussen 24 juni en 9 september 1751 regelmatig met deze concertserie.

24 juli 1751

De Heeren de Graf en Michelet, Meesters op de Viool, Clavier en Dwars-Fluyt, zullen den 27 July, 's avonds ten 6 uuren Concert geven, in de Witte Moolen op den Cingel, alwaer ook Lootjes te bekomen zyn; een Heer met een Dame be aeld ƒ 1 : 10.

27 juli 1751

By J. Smit Boek- en Muziekverkoper in de Pylsteeg by de Warmoesstraet t'Amsterd., is gedrukt en te bekomen, de Nieuwe Hollandsche SCHOUWBURG, zynde een verzameling van verscheyde Serieuse en Pluggedansen, die op de Viool, Dwarsfluyt, Hoboo, Chalumeau, Clavier en andere Muziek Instrumenten gespeeld konnen werden, tot gebruyk der Leerlingen opgesteld, zeer net in het koper gegraveert; de prys is 17 st. en in een bantje ƒ 1. By bovengem. zyn veele andere van de beste Muziek-werken te bekomen.

Op 6 januari 1752 wordt het tweede deel aangekondigd: *'Dit Deeltje bestaet in 60 Dansen, zynde alle nieuw en nooit in Druk geweest; alle geestig en vrolijk door een voornaem Muzikant tot gebruyk der Leerlingen opgesteld.'*

26 oktober 1751

Op heden word uitgegeven: Het Maendelyks Musikaels Tydverdryf, bestaende in nieuwe Hollandse Canzonetten of Zangliederen, op de Italiaense trant in 't Musiek gebragt, met een Basso-Continuo daer onder, mede zeer bequaem om op de Clavecimbael, Viool, Dwarsfluyt, Hoboë en andere Instrumenten gespeelt te werden; kost 24 stuyv. Van dit Werkje, dat zeer cierlyk in 't koper gesneden is, en niet alleen tot vermaek, maer ook tot nut voor Leerlinge opgesteld is, zal alle maenden een Vervolg werden uitgegeven t'Amsterd. by A. OLOFSEN Boekverkoper. daer ook de volgende nieuwe Werken te bekomen zyn, als: A. MAHAUT, VI Sinfonie a piu stromenti, a 6 gl. VI Sonaten a Tré, a 4 gl. En VI Sonaten a due Tilauti Travr. o due Violini, a 50 stuyv. alle met Privilegie. Nog F. G. MICHELET, III Sonaten per il Cembalo, a 30 stuyv. Italiaense Zangduetten, a 2 gl. En een Verzameling van nieuwe serieuse, Comique, Boere- en Contre-dansen, Menuetten en andere Airs, met een Basso Continuo daer onder, a 24 st.

6 juni 1752

By J. COVENS Junior, Boekverkoper t'Amsterdam op den Vygendam werd uitgegeven, Tercetti per il Cimbalo con il Flauto Travesiere o sia Violino da Sr. Santo Lapis, à 4 gulden.

11 november 1752

A. OLOFSEN t'Amft., heeft gedrukt ARONDEUS nut en dienftig Zang-Boekje, zynde de eerfte Vaerfen der Pfalmen en Geeftelyke Liederen, met een cierlyke Noor, benevens 25 Vercier-Kransjes om op de Muzykwerken te konnen plakken, en ftaet in korten uyt te komen C. F. HURLEBUSCH 2 van zyn 6 ITALIAENSE ARIAES; als mede J. N. LENTZ Concerto per il Cembalo Concertato; item de 2 deelen XII Sonaten van de beroemde TARTINI, als mede te bekomen alle de werken van ELSLAND, COUWENBERG en VERMOTEN, waer in uytmunten de Geboorte- Kruys- en Liefdens-Gezangen, benevens Gelynde Muzykpapieren.
De nieuwe Muzykwerken gemaekt door die met de daed beroemde Compofiteurs, zyn heden t'Amfterd. by A. Oloffen en in de andere fteden by de Heeren Organiften, Muzykmeefters en Boekverkopers te bekomen, als: Ant. Mahaut XII Sonaten, Duerten, in 2 Deelen, voor de Fluto Travers; item de 9 cierlyk uitgevoerde Hollandfe Canzonnetten, met een Regifter, berymt door den Heer K. Elzevier, fo als ook een Italiaenfche Canzounet in 't zelve formaet; als mede de VI Sinfonyen en VI Sonaten, Trioos van gem. Autheur; item de 2 Deelen Verzamelingen van Comique, Boere en Contra-danffen &c., als mede 2 Deelen Diveriffement Theatrales; nog 3 Sonaten door Gerard Vos, Organift van de Lutherfe Kerk tot Rotterdam; de pryzen, volgens Catalogus (van m. er andere beroemde Mannen) zyn om niet te bekomen.

11 januari 1753

De Muficq Lievende werd bekend gemaekt dat by Joh. Covens Junior, Boekverkoper t'Amft. op den Vygendam, werd uytgegeeven Amufemens Agreables dedié au beau fexe ou Receuil des Chanfonnettes Francoifes mis en Mufique dans le Gout Italien par A. Mahaut. Dit Werkje beftaet in 12 Franfe Chanzonetten of Zangliederen opgefteld tot nut der Leerlingen en vermaak der Liefhebbers, en kan meede voor de Clavercimbael, Dwarsfluyt, Vioolen andere Inftrumenten gebruykt worden, a 24 ftuyv. By den zelven zyn meede te bekomen A. Mahaut VI Sinfonie a 6 guld. A. Mahaut VI. Sonate a tre due Flanti Traverfi o due Violini c B. C. a 4 guld. Hamal VI. Sinfonie a due Violini, Alto Violale B.C. a f 5: 5; zyn mede te bekomen in de andere fteden by de Heeren Organiften en Muficqmrs.

25 september 1753

t'Amft. by Joh. Covens Junior, op den Vygendam word op heeden uitgegeeven, Ant. Mahaut Opera IV. Lib. 1. VI. Sonate a Due Flauti Traverfierl o Due Violini a f 2: - 10: - als meede het 2de ftukje van Les Amufemens Agreables, ou Chanfonnettes Francoifes dans le gout Italien, door dezelve Autheur a f 1: -: 4 -

22 augustus 1754

t'Amft. by A. Oloffen, en alom ter plaetze waer de Conditien te bekomen zyn, kan men tot ultimo Augufty nog inteekenen In het bekende en beroemde Werk van J.J. QUANTZ uyt het Hoogduyts vertaeld door den Muficale Taelkenner J. W. Luft g, waer van de afleevering fo prompt zal gefchieden als dat van Sr. 8r. Lapis: by gem. Oloffenfen by den Autheur H. RADEKER, is te bekomen Opera Terza tr Sonate per il Cimbalo con Violino Obligato a f 3, en 2 Werkjes voor de Fluto Tra. ieder 20 ft.

De eerste advertentie van Olofsen ter intekening op het boek van Quantz verscheen op 13 augustus 1754. Op 14 januari 1755 wordt het verschijnen van het boek aangekondigd:
'By A. OLOFSEN, t'Amst. en alom in d'andere steden, werd heden uitgegeven grondig onderwys van den aard en regte behandeling der DWARSFLUIT, treffelyke Regelenschat der COMPOSITIE en uitvoeringe der voornaamste Muzykstukken op de gebruikelykste Instrumenten, zo in Italien, Vrankryk als Duitsland, door lange ondervindinge en schrandere opmerking by een verzameld, door den beroemden Compositeur J.J. QUANTZ, Kamermusicus van syn Koningl. Maj. van Pruissen, uit t'Hoogduits vertaeld door J.W. LUSTIG, Organist en Compositeur tot Groningen; kost 't groot pap. 6 gl. en 't kl. pap. 5 gl. zo als 's Vertaalders beide Werken over de Muzyk en Musicaale Spraekkunde byeen kosten 3 guld.'

5 februari 1757

J. J. HUMMEL, Muzyk-verkoper t'Amfterdam, geeft heden uyt VI. Sonate à Due Flauti Traverfieri & Baffo di A'berto Groneman, Opera Seconda à f 3; dit Werk kan met en zonder de Bas gefpeeld worden. Degiardini Overtures voor Violins en andere Inft. à f 12. Pieces Choifies pour le Clav. à f 1: 5, gem. en zyne Coresp. geven heden gratis uyt, Conditien van Inteekeninge voor XII. Odes D'Horace, overgezet in Italiaenfe Cantates, dit Werk zal in de maend van Maert in Londen uytkomen; breeder in de Conditien te zien, de lentek. penningen worden eerft by ontfangft van het Werk betaelt, ook zyn by hem alle foorten van Viool en Bas-Snaeren, in paquets voor een civiele prys te bekomen.

118

9 augustus 1757

Op heden werd t'Amft. by A. Oloffen, zo ook alom uitgegeven de Mufikaale Lente- en Somer-Tydverdryf, gecomponeerd door A. Mahaut en in Digtmaat die beroemde Compofitie door de Heer Korn. Elzevier, welke 2 ftukjes by een in 36 Neerduitfe Zang-Ariaas beftaan, om voor alle Inftrumenten te konnen gefpeelt werden, koften 2 gl., het 3de en 4de zal op zyn tyd, ieder om eene gulde, zo als VI Sonaten voor 3 Fluto Traverfen in 2 Deelen voor 3 gl. te bekomen zyn.

28 september 1758

Geduurende de Kermis, zal t'Amft. ten huize van ANTHONY BERGMEYER, Caftelyn in BLAAUW JAN, te zien zyn een overheerlyk KONST-KABINET, benevens 2 nieuw geinventeerde Mechanifche FIGUUREN, verbeeldende een HERDER en HERDERIN, welke op een natuurlyke wys op de Fluit-Traverfiere fpeelen, Primo en Secondo, wiens weerga nooit meer te zien is geweeft, men betaald voor de 1fte plaats 6 ftuiv. en voor de 2de 3 ft. Ook zal aldaar op de Publyke Plaats, geduurende gem. tyd te zien zyn extra fraay Vee, wiens gelyke van fchoonheid, hier te land, nooit meer zyn te zien geweeft.

16 december 1758

Werd bekent gemaakt aan alle Heeren en Dames, als dat op de Jooden Breedftraat by de St. Anthonyfluis, in het Jonge Gekroonde Schaap, zal heden zynde Saturdag werden CONCERT gehouden, daar zig zal laten hooren Mr. Ifa Gerfonie, primo Violift met Solos en Concerte, en zyn Neef Abr. Gerfonie, met Solos en Concerte op de Bas, en Mr: Apking, zal zig laten horen op de Fluit-Travers, en een Italiaanfe Zangeres zal Zingen; Saturdags, Maandags en Donderdags 's avonds ten 6 uuren.

26 december 1758

By Johannes Smit, Boekverkoper, op de Fluwele Burgwal by de Halfteeg, zyn te bekomen fix Sonata a duo Violini, getrokken uit 12 Opera Arien f 1-16, het zelve werk voor 2 Dwarsfluiten f 1-14, fix Sonates a duo Flauti Travers a Baffo Continus di Befocci f 2-8, 12 Sonates da Cimbalo di Piano & Forte detto Volgarmento di Martelliti, de Hollandfche Schouwburg voor de Viool en Dwarsfluit tot gebruik der Leerlingen, 4 Deelen f 3-8, elk deel apart 17 fluivers.

22 september 1759

By A. OLOFSEN, t'Amft., is, gelyk mede in de andere fteden by de Boekverkopers, Organiften, en Muzikmeefters, te bekomen, de 2 eerfte Sinfonye van de groote Compofiteurs Graun en Tubel, met dubbelde Baffen, Walthoorns en Hoboen, a f 2-10; zullende de 2 andere van Wagenfeil en Stamitz, ultimo October tot dezelfde prys volgen, en vervolgens van 6 tot 6 weeken de 2 den van deze 1ften, zonder iets voorui't te verzoeken; item III Sonaten Trios voor de Dwarsfluit, Violen en Cembalo van F. X. Richter op 16 Plaaten a f 2-10; nog van le Buntini XII kleine Sonaatjes, 2 Delen f 2-10, ieder VI apart a 25 fluiv.; nog een Difcipel Werkje van 't Savoiaarts Meisje met het Marmotje, beftaande in Vatiatien, Menuetten en Polonoiffen, ligt en aardige Voifen a 14 ftuyv. Gemelde Oloffen is door inkoop magtig alle de Exemplaren van Jozzi zyn 8 Clavier-Sonaten, koft f 3-10.

7 februari 1760

By A. OLOFSEN, t'Amft., zo ook by die in andere Couranten gemeld worden, is te bekomen de eerfte Sinfonyen van Steinmetz en Wagenfeil, met Fluto Traverfen en Walthoorn, ieder 25 ft.; item een nieuw Stukie voor alle Inftrumenten, gecompyneert van 16 Opera Ariaas, 1fte Deel, waar onder 5 der Franfe Opera, de Ninette à la Coeur, en 2 der befte andere Operaas, 't 2de ftaat in 't kort te volgen en is reeds dat van de Cervante Maitreffe onder dat Stukie begrepen, niet minder cierlyk dan het eerfte, zal ook tot 24 ft. alomme by gem. te bekomen zyn; als ook de 2de Trios voor Fluto Traverfen en Bas, door A. Coeb.

22 november 1760

t'Amft. by J. J. Hummel, is gedrukt en word op heeden (zo als ook by B. Hummel in 's Hage,) uitgegeven, Mr. A. MAHAUT, nieuwe manier om binnen korten tyd op de Dwarsfluit te leeren fpeelen, tot gebruik van aanvangers en meer gevorderde opgefteld, voorzien met 12 Nooten Tabulaas, dit Werkje is op de eene zyde Franfch en de andere Duitfch, en koft f 1-16; NB. In dit kort en grondig Boekje zullen de Liefhebbers vinden al wat op de Dwarsfluit ter uitvoering kan gebragt worden; verders C. WAGENSEIL VI. Cembalo Sonaten Opera I., nieuwlyks in Londen gedrukt a f 3; G. FRITZ VI. Sonate à Due Violini a f 2-10; nevens een nieuwe Mufick Catalogus gratis.

Op 18 november 1760 verscheen een advertentie met dezelfde tekst.

Publishers, Editors, Editions and Urtexts

Frans Vester

The way in which historical music is notated (tempo indications in relation to note values and time signatures, presence or absence of marks of articulation, dynamics, etc.) has its own meaning that sometimes is not immediately apparent. Therefore, the musician who wishes to perform a piece of music from the past must have a certain familiarity with the notation to be able to make a guess at deciphering it. The possibility of success is conceivable only with the help of a correct edition, one which reproduces the text as it was originally handed down, and that is neither 'revised', 'improved', nor otherwise mutilated. Such an edition, then, may not contain any inauthentic articulations, dynamics, fingerings, bowings, breathing marks, cuts, written-out ornaments or similar bits of 'indoctrination', unless the editor considers such alterations or additions unavoidable. In that case, they must be rendered clearly recognizable as such by means of smaller or italic type, brackets, dotted slurs, or explanation in a foreword. It is deplorable that this is not as yet general policy.
Hereafter, we shall not concern ourselves with the musical significance of the notation itself, but primarily with the quality of the edition, which must in no way form an obstacle to the correct interpretation of the music.

The person responsible for the edition is the publisher, who for centuries has been the most important distributor of music and the primary link between composer and performer. In the case of contemporary music (regardless of the period), problems between composer and publisher do not usually arise, since for the most part they are in close contact. However, the situation changes completely with the publication of music from an earlier period. Since the middle of the previous century, which saw a revival of interest in 18th-century music, publishers have occupied themselves with the publication of new editions. As direct contact with the composer was not possible, collaboration with an editor, who, as it were, represented the composer, was necessary. Because the first editors and musicians of the period were initially lacking in historical knowledge of the 18th century, and indeed considered such knowledge largely superfluous (after all, as it was a century later they reasoned that they were a century wiser), the first editions were heavily edited, unaccompanied by commentaries and bore all too clearly the stamp of the 19th century. Moreover, they often had little to do with the original composition. These 'pre-interpreted', 'modernized' editions, whose distance from the original source was not apparent, were accepted without question. It is unfortunate that, to some extent, this is still done today.

The first 19th-century practical editions of baroque and classical flute music were produced with the assistance of editors, for example: the Sonatas of J.S. Bach (Peters, 1865, editors F. David and F. Hermann) and the Concerti of Mozart (Breitkopf & Härtel, 1884, editor C. Burchard). At the time of publication, these two editions could be compared, if so desired, with the already published *Gesamtausgaben* of the respective composers. As is generally known, these *Gesamtausgaben* contain no additions or alterations which are not recognizable as such; they reproduce the so-called *Urtext*. Most of the 18th-century flute repertoire published in the first half of the 20th century was not available in *Gesamtausgaben*, making comparison impossible. The earlier 20th-century editions, in particular, are full of octave transpositions, altered notes and additional or changed indications of articulation and dynamics. Continuo parts are realized as complex piano accompaniments[1]. The editors did not hesitate to interchange the flute and piano (right-hand) parts for a number of bars at a time.[2] This is unscrupulous behavior with respect to the composer, but the editors, who knew no better, cannot really be held responsible.

With the course of time, fortunately, the historical insight of editors has improved, and a number of publishers have made use of the resulting changes in editing. It is still a lamentable fact that the great majority of publishers, even today, continue to distribute badly edited editions of old music without a word of explanation. This is particularly true of nearly all American and most French publishers.

The first (and for the time being, the last?) edition of Poulenc's Sonata (Chester) is a brand-new example of unfortunate publishing policy. At the head of the flute part, we read: 'The flute part has been revised by Jean-Pierre Rampal'. This is probably the first time in the history of music publishing that the first edition of a composition by a — then, in 1958 — living composer has appeared with an edited flute part. Even the permission of the composer is not a valid argument for not printing the original flute part (if only in the piano score). We are given no explanation of the why and wherefore of the whole procedure, let alone any information as to the whereabouts of the autograph. We can only guess.[3]

A bad edition, when unavoidable for lack of a better one, is not only useless but insulting. After all, the editor apparently considers us incapable of arriving at our own interpretation. On the contrary, we are more or less obliged to accept his condescension. A bad editor leaves the musician with the impression that he stands in quicksand. What did the composer write? What was the editor's contribution? Was there any contribution? If so, what and where? This kind of editing, moreover, makes it commercially difficult, sometimes even impossible, for a conscientious publisher to produce a correct edition; unknowing flutist X, who already has an edition 'revised' by famous flutist Y, will think twice before purchasing a reliable edition made by unknown editor Z.

In the light of all this, it is clear that an *Urtext* edition, when available, is preferable to any other modern edition. When this is not the case and one is forced to make use of a doubtful edition, then it is worthwhile — in fact, one is morally obligated towards the composer — to acquire copies of the autograph, of an old manuscript, or of an old edition. If it is possible to find a facsimile of the autograph or study the autograph itself, then there are no more obstacles between performer and music. The musician is, so to speak, eye to eye with the composer, and no publisher can compete with that.

Unfortunately, we cannot uncritically accept even the most ambitiously planned *Gesamtausgaben* (*Urtext* editions) or semi-*Urtexts*. Although the editor may adhere strictly to the *Editionsrichtlinien* (Editors' directives) laid down for him, he sometimes encounters problems for which there are only imperfect solutions. He can explain and justify these in the *Kritischer Bericht* (Editorial notes), which is intended for the performer. Frequently it is a case of unclear indications of rhythm, notes, dynamics, and accidentals which are susceptible to varying interpretations. In addition, it is not always easy to find a good basis for an *Urtext* edition. There are neither autographs nor old printed editions in existence for the flute sonatas in E minor and E major (BWV 1034 and 1035) by J.S. Bach. For BWV 1035, the oldest written copies were used for the various *Urtexts*, but these all date from around or after 1800, some sixty years after the date of composition. A note on one of these copies says that it was taken from the autograph which Bach brought with him on his visit to Potsdam in 1747; the copy is supposed to have been made for the chamberlain, Fredersdorf.[4] All of this sounds trustworthy, but the articulation signs, which seem to have originated with the copyist rather than the composer, remain doubtful when compared with existing works of Bach in autograph. Hans-Peter Schmitz's suggestion that we take these markings as examples for Bach's other flute music therefore seems questionable.[5]

Various randomly chosen examples of human error and incorrect text interpretation from the *Neue Bach Ausgabe* (NBA), from a semi-*Urtext* edition by Bärenreiter (F. Kuhlau, Fantasie op. 38/1), and the *Neue Schubert Ausgabe* (NSA), will serve to show that an *Urtext* edition is not infallible. The examples are intended to impress upon the reader the need for caution.

J.S. Bach, Sonata in B minor BWV 1030, first movement, bar 58 (flute part)

in NBA:

in autograph:[6]

An error in the rhythmic notation which is found not only in the NBA, but also in all other printed editions originates with an uncorrected misprint in the *Bach Gesellschaft Ausgabe* (BGA), which also served as the *Grundlage* (groundwork) for the NBA. The misprint has once again escaped the attention of the editor; as a result, there is no comment in the *Kritischer Bericht*.

J.S. Bach, Sonata BWV 1030, second movement, bar 6 (fl)

in NBA:

in BGA:

in autograph:[6]

Bach followed the procedure of his time: an accidental is valid only for the note which it precedes. Otherwise, why would he repeat the ♯ three times in this bar? Not until much later was the rule established that an accidental remains valid until the end of the bar unless cancelled by a ♮. As a rule, the ♮ was used in Baroque notation only to cancel a key signature. In modern notation, therefore, the bar should read:

In bar 13 (fl) we encounter a similar error. Here too, the last g♯² in the bar should be a g². Neither of these details is mentioned in the *Kritischer Bericht*.

J.S. Bach, Sonata BWV 1030, second movement, bars 5, 6, 7, 8, 11, 12, 13, 15 (fl): beaming of the notes and the direction of note stems in the autograph differ from those in the NBA. As an example, bar 5:

in NBA:

in autograph:[6]

In these cases, the problems originate with the publisher, who requires the editor to conform to the customs of modern notation. The performer who is sensitive to delicate nuances and who, for example, might wish to use the beaming of the notes as an indication for phrasing, feels somehow deprived by the NBA. Neither the beaming nor direction of note stems is referred to in the *Kritischer Bericht*.

In the Domine Deus of the Mass in B minor BWV 232, the first bar of the flute part reads as follows in the score:

Markings by Bach in the separate flute part transform this into a Lombardic rhythm:

A performance indication of this importance, originating with the composer, should have been reported in the *Kritischer Bericht*. That this was not done is, bibliographically speaking, probably correct, but unacceptable in terms of performance practice.

In the semi-*Urtext* edition of Kuhlau's Fantasie op. 38/1 for solo flute (Bärenreiter BA 3323, editor M. Gümbel), human error must be held accountable. Bars 9, 10, 11 and 12 have been omitted from the Ariette con variazioni. They read:

In conclusion, a few examples from the Variations pour le Pianoforte et Flûte op. 160 by Schubert. The composer wrote 'decresc.' in bar 11 (fl) of the introduction and later crossed it out. It is a passage where the player would tend to make a decrescendo even if the indication were not there. Might this not be an indication for the performer? Not one single edition mentions this detail in the accompanying notes (if there are any).

Bars 319 and 320 (fl) read as follows in the autograph:

The same passage in the NSA (Kassel, 1970):

The word 'simile' should in this case have been placed between brackets to make it clear that it does not originate with Schubert, but was added by the editor. In addition, the indication (one slur to the bar) cannot be literally correct. It is more probable that Schubert intended something like:

In this case, Nikolaus Delius's *Revidierte Ausgabe* (Breitkopf & Härtel, nr 6658, 1971) is the only trustworthy edition.

Bars 322 and 337 are more complicated. Delius has not read bar 322 (fl) carefully enough in the autograph.[7] His edition gives it as:

Bar 337, in contrast:

This is, putting aside the question of misinterpretation of the text, an improbable reading, since it concerns a passage of seven bars which is repeated in identical form (bars 319-325 and 334-340). In both the NSA and the autograph, bars 322 and 337 are identical. They read:

But the NSA is nonetheless at fault here, because Schubert's notation has not been correctly modernized. For Schubert, a ♮ cancelling an alteration indicated in the key signature is valid, as with Bach, only for the note which it precedes. In other words, the reading of both bars (322 and 337) is that of bar 337 as given in Delius.

A final example:

Bar 264 (Var. VI) in the autograph contains a slip of the pen in the piano part (RH). This bar reads:

Schubert neglected to correct this error (sixteenth-note beam on second chord RH). All the published editions interpret this as if he had forgotten to dot the notes of the first chord. But this does not agree with the context of the passage. Flute and piano (RH) parts are in consistent rhythmic agreement. Moreover, the published reading creates the following relationship between the flute part and the middle voice of the piano's right hand:

which can hardly be what was intended.[8]
All the other editions contain so many errors in both flute and piano parts that they are virtually unusable.

It is encouraging that not only more and more *Urtext* editions, but also other valuable editions are currently becoming available. These are primarily the numerous facsimile editions of flute music (particularly early prints) from the first half of the 18th century (SPES, UCP, Afour Editions, EMF, Mark Meadow, etc.). They have certain drawbacks for the amateur. The continuo parts are, of course, unrealized, the type face is frequently different from that in current use, and a number of prints make use of the French violin clef.

These drawbacks are not present in what might be called an 'ideal edition', such as that made (against all expectations) by Leduc. This publisher has brought out editions of the Sonata op. 9/2 by Leclair (1977) and the Sonata op. 2/2 by Blavet (1978), both for flute and continuo. These editions consist of a realized score, separate flute and continuo parts, and a reduced facsimile of the first printed edition. The example has been followed by Amadeus, who has produced similar editions of the Solo Sonata of C.P.E. Bach and the Partita of J.S. Bach. This rather expensive editing procedure deserves a far wider currency; it would enable everyone to form an independent basis for interpretation.

Notes

1 See, for example, J.B. Loeillet, Sonatas and Trio Sonatas (Lemoine, 1911, editor A. Béon).

2 See, for example, L. van Beethoven, Sonata in B♭ major (Zimmerman, editor A. van Leeuwen) and — a much later edition — Mozart, Sonatas KV 10-15 (Edition Reinhardt, 1959, editor Joseph Bopp).

3 The autograph is in the Library of Congress, Washington, D.C.

4 NBA: Hans-Peter Schmitz, *Kritischer Bericht*, Werke für Flöte, Serie VI, Band 3.

5 Foreword by Hans-Peter Schmitz in J.S. Bach, Flute Sonatas, Kassel, Bärenreiter, 1966.

6 Cf. the facsimile edition of the Bach-Archiv, Leipzig 1961.

7 Delius, incidentally is not the only one to make this mistake. See, for example, the Peters edition and the old Breitkopf & Härtel edition, both of which contain the same error.

8 The reverse of this mistake is found in J.S. Bach's Partita BWV 1013. Bar 34 of the Bourrée Anglaise, in the manuscript, shows an unclear mark after the third eighth note which could be read as a dot, but the fourth note is also an eighth note rather than a sixteenth. All editions (including the NBA) give the rhythm of this bar incorrectly as ♫ ♪. It should be: ♫ ♫

Translation: David Shapero